DROPPING WOOD, SPILLING WATER

DROPPING WOOD, SPILLING WATER

ILLNESS, DISABILITY, AND AGING AS PATHS FOR CONSCIOUSNESS AND BEING

ROBERT SHUMAN

2017
Gratitude Books
drshuman@gmail.com

ORDER OF SELECTIONS

Thanks Giving   vii

Hmmmm…   xi

The First Initiation   1
  Everything Depends on Everything Else   4
  My Diagnosis, 1979–1982   7
  A Painful Difference   12
  We Don't Suffer from Diseases   15
  A World Unmade   17
  The Expectable Unexpected   20

Everyday Life   23
  The "I" Becomes One Thing, Our Bodies Another   27
  The Texture of Time   33
  Life Is Suffering   36
  We Flee from Sadness   40

Defense Mechanisms   45
  Denial and False Pride   48
  Guilt   52
  Practice Makes…   54
  Sloth   56
  Schadenfreude   60
  The Limit of Our Being   64
  Coils of the Serpent of Despair   66

The Second Initiation   69
  When the Call Comes   69
  Crisis of Consciousness   73

Taking Responsibility   76

Creating a New Geography   79

Wholly Breath   82

Things That Go Bump in the Night   88

Turn the Other Cheek   91

A Slip of Mind   94

Will and Wish   96

Creativity and Illness   101

MS Is My Muse   101

We Do Not Live by Bread Alone   104

Art as Healer   110

The Estuary   113

The Portuguese Man of War   115

Death   121

Drop the Cursed Pettiness   121

Impermanence, Compassion, and Mr. Holmes   124

There Is No Map for Grief   125

So Glad to Cry   128

Ali, "a Truly Free Man of Faith"   131

Old and New   134

All Illness Is Family Business   137

The Yoke of Relationship   137

Burdens of Care   140

Family Ethics   143

We Are Not Rational Actors   147

The So-Called "Well Spouse"   150

Is Love Just a Four-Letter Word?   157

THANKS GIVING

O NE OF THE greatest blessings of thanks giving is the opportunity it offers me to express gratitude for how well and with so much joy I have spent the last 38 years since the symptoms of MS first appeared. First to thank, of course, is Sheila—lover, friend, and wife for 50 years—generous, beautiful, gifted, enduring more than her due with grace, patience, and far less complaint, irritation, or despair than is rightly hers.

My children, Daniel and Rebecca, each in a personal and particular manner, have without shame and with care helped me participate as much as possible (and tolerable) in the lives of their families, as have their kind partners, Anna and Paul. The time and love Papa has been given with and by my grandchildren—beautiful, bright, determined Maddy, 15; always lively, creative, film and video actor and maker Ben, 13; Caito, 3, angelic hair and nature, my go-to guy for all things truck; and smiling new boy, Jonah, 6 months—all an unending source of unconditional pleasure and determination to live on with zest and laughter.

My mother gives willingly and goes far out of her way to visit and does whatever she is able to make our lives easier. My dear dogs, Bodhi and Kai, devoted companions, getting me moving no matter what, are spirit beings to me. My wonderful loyal friends for years have not only put up with the difficult logistics and tolerated postponements and cancellations to get together for meals, movies, and conversations, but do much more than they ought to ensure that we meet.

My extraordinarily competent and wise physical therapist, Wendy, with humor and warmth has made it possible to function better and avoid worse for years. My physician, Dr. Raizin, trusts and supports me to get the medical care I need as soon as possible. My clients move me with their confidence in me that they bring to our sessions; the insights into their lives that they share have aided me with my own. My painting teachers, Jack and Deborah, brought me an immeasurable gift.

And special thanks to Perry McIntosh, friend for nearly 50 years, who gets it, and without whom, nothing done.

And to many, many more unnamed, some forgotten, but all worthy of thanks. And to the Holy Breath which continues to give me life neither deserved nor earned, but to which I owe all…

and I'm so glad
Yes, I'm so glad
I'm so glad
So glad
I want to thank You,

Hmmmm…

I WAS A bit taken aback one evening not long ago, just a few days before the winter solstice and the various celebrations around the globe that welcome the return of a little light to what seems an ever-darkening world, when my wife and I were at dinner with another couple. "To health!" the fellow toasted. Sitting in my wheelchair, I raised my glass as well but, "Hmmm," I thought, "why to health?" If I were to identify values that are at least as important as health, my long list would include beauty, friendship, love, wisdom, gratitude, courage, truth, or simplicity. Yet with the possible exception of friendship, our glass is rarely raised to these equally worthy goods. Why health?

Assuming he meant physical health, I'd place this toast in the same category as "to prosperity" or "to a long life," which to me salute economic security and sufficient time to enjoy and repay the gift of life. But if the toast is to health because physical illness is viewed as intrinsically bad, I object.

After all, what is health? Its original meanings gather around wholeness, not healing, but holy and sacred as well. To be *ill*, on the other hand, perhaps not surprisingly, appears only as far back as 1200 meaning malevolent, evil, unfortunate, bad. But surely healthy people are not particularly holy, nor those of us who are ill notably wicked. Might it, in fact, in quite a reversal, be possible to use illness as a way toward greater consciousness in the service of decent values? The toast and my silent reflection upon it were a miniature replay of the question asked by generations of philosophers: "What is the good life?" Is physical health one of the conditions necessary to pursue our cherished aims and goals? Since most of us will experience illness or some degree of disability as we age, is the good life limited to only our peak years or enjoyed by only the fortunate, perpetually healthy few? No. As our bodies fall apart, we don't stop living. Ill or not, we are all in the same boat. Although death surely comes, we don't rush to greet him; we keep pursuing our desires.

When I was much younger, I spent 14 years after a college span of "sixties seeking" associated with a community, a teacher, and a tradition for the purpose of "waking up" from the semi-consciousness in which we ordinarily pass our lives. In 1982, I met with a wise friend and professor from my university days. He was intimately familiar with the path I was on and had also conducted ethnographic research on similarities and contrasts between Western and non-Western psychologies, healings, and spiritual practices and paths.

"I hear you've been diagnosed with MS," he affirmed with concern after our warm reunion. "I think you no longer need this 'work,'" he said with a serious smile. "You now have what it was to provide. You have found what you're looking for." And as in so many tales of old, he disappeared, leaving me with a question, a map, and a mission: to find the treasure in front of me.

I have found that treasure. And the treasure is my teacher and healer. Not, however, the positive-thinking, disease-slaying hero who lives in the dualistic paradigm of sickness and cure. The healer is the illness experience itself, fragmented, uncertain, and bearing suffering. The essential "me-ness" of my nature remains. I live without, from within.

In fact, with allowances for aging—a condition we all share—from my point of view my life is better. I am reminded that in the central narratives of many religious traditions, it is often that which is most despised or vulnerable—the outlaw Moses, the hunted infant Jesus—that is the source of new spirit and hope. And the messenger of hope and spirit (Elijah the Passover guest, or in Muslim tradition Khidr, the Green

Man) is often invisible or disguised. "If you meet Buddha on the road, kill him," not only suggests that his being is within us, but also that we can never know in what person or situation we might find wisdom, help, or dharma.

It is now more than 30 years since my diagnosis of multiple sclerosis. Occasional stumbles, trips, and falls have given way to a cane, then a walker, and now a wheelchair full time. My MS is not cured; no symptoms have disappeared and some have worsened, but all are manageable with a variety of interventions. Many activities I enjoyed before my diagnosis are no longer available to me. But for a variety of reasons, my life is not worse than it was in 1982. In fact, I describe my health, as do many of us with illness, as good. My path toward healing and making a richer life from the stuff of suffering continues.

What awaits you as you enter these pages is a series of reflections that encompasses one year of living with my chronic illness—multiple sclerosis, diagnosed nearly forty years ago—and its effects upon my family, in particular my "well partner" caregiver and my wife of five decades, Sheila. I think you will find value in this collection; even if only a few paragraphs are helpful I shall be glad. My experience of illness is influenced by a half century of study and work with traditions of consciousness, as well as my practice as a psychotherapist. Regardless of diagnosis or degree of disability and while still acknowledging our differences, those of us who suffer anguish of the body have much in common.

The courses of any two chronic illnesses or human afflictions are not the same. There were no maps to lead me to the territory I discovered and continue to explore, nor does the route I sketch match up to the land through which you journey. We find ourselves where we are, and when we look carefully we see more or less than we thought we knew. But perhaps some of the features I have found and how I make my way through the terrain of illness may be useful to you.

It is also true that I know enough about you to know we share a great deal. In fact, there is very little of importance about me that you do not know, and I possess a nearly complete in-depth picture of you as well. How strange that we often find ourselves ignorant of one another. How is this possible? We think of ourselves as individuals with unique characteristics. We imagine we contain a secret self, one that commits acts of which we are secretly ashamed or proud and harbors fantasies and unspoken desires. We disguise ourselves with a personality that is often at odds with the autonomous, anonymous self we believe hides behind it.

Maybe we each think of our invisible "me" as an aspect of soul, unknowable, *terra incognita* to even our most precious lovers' enduring and discerning regard. But we are not solitary souls dwelling in well-defended, skin-wrapped castles. We each know the most important facts about one another, objective facts that dwarf any subjective ones that we assume define any one of us.

This I affirm: We are each thrown into this world, to parents, family, society, and culture, with genetic endowments, economic standing, and in many circumstances, all without any choice on our part. Also, each of our bodies is subject to aging, illness, injury, and, most importantly, death. I know this about me and, with identical assurance, about you.

Secondly, as Buddha realized and I admit about myself and, yes, about you: We suffer due to our attachment to the belief, conscious or not, that we can avoid these **fundamental facts**. I know that I, and likely you as well, cling to hopes that enough learning or war or meditation or sex or health or happiness or math or music or wealth or power or having can help us avoid the reality of the "date expired" timestamp of being human.

Generally, even if we mean radically different things by the words, we prefer kindness to cruelty, beauty to ugliness, creation to destruction. When we see red, does each of us identify the same color? In general, the answer is probably "close enough," if we pose the question functionally. More importantly, I think, is that I know you most likely have and use the word *red* for a range of colors that you perceive. So we share color, music, movement, rhythm. The particular meanings we assign these terms may matter greatly, but at least it's a starting point for understanding. We have so much in common. The breath from my words and the light reflected off you to my eyes literally enter and change me. The speed with which a spontaneous conversation between two strangers can spiral into a joyful dance of ideas demonstrates how much intuitive knowledge we share of each other.

The reflections in this book are presented in several sections divided roughly by themes. Yet the biological, sociological, familial, psychological, and spiritual effects that are present with our afflictions are so organic and interactive that one piece could easily have been placed in a different section or even sprinkled among several. That's the nature of both chronic illness and paths of consciousness and spirit. It is hard to define how one symptom affects others or even to distinguish particular symptoms from emotions, just as it is not easy to discern how any one aspect of "conscious" work influences a manifestation of our being.

Paths exist, but we make them our own as we take them, lingering or turning, stepping or stopping here or there. The word *dharma* is rooted far in the past to words for carry, horse tack, and harmony. Dharma suggests to me not a rigid teaching or set of rules, but ideas that helps us find our own way of guiding body and mind through the world, gracefully, secure, alert. My practice, way, or dharma, if you will, to live more consciously is, in fact, my illness, increasing disability, and accompanying aging. My way, if you will, reminds me of the walks I took with my beloved Tibetan Terrier, Bodhi, for whom I wrote this poem:

Origami of Time

We walk, Bodhi and I.
We stroll through Birch, Cedar, Linden,
Cherry, Oak and Maple.
He marks trees along our way
as I leave these marks to you.
He plows the past up with his nose,
paws loosening scents of other beings
and waves his muzzle to the wind.
Perfect companion, my Tibetan,
turning the smell of was into is.

The vocabularies of medicine, pain, disease, cure, and suffering constitute the few remaining languages through which our culture can struggle with the facts of affliction, healing, and meaning and where they fit in the order and disorder of self and life. In this book, I hope to bring illness out from its isolation within the medical setting, where it is often subordinated to our cultural ideals of wellness and health.

When we are given a diagnosis of chronic illness we are also presented with an initiation into one, or possibly two new worlds. Traditional initiations involve movement through stages that lead to a significant change of role and status. They lead to separation, removing us from everyday life and a passage to earned knowledge that places greater responsibility on us upon our return to serve our families and communities with greater maturity and compassion.

A colleague who works with children with juvenile diabetes and their families was asked by a urologist to speak to a group of men recently diagnosed with prostate cancer. When she protested that she knew nothing about the disease, the physician remarked, "So what? You can give them hope." He knew that her ability and experience helping people cope with newly threatened worlds were more important than her knowledge or expertise with a particular medical diagnosis. Healers are people who can make a difference in another person's world to lessen suffering, restore morale, and relieve pain. And so we may be healers as we are ill.

When chronic illness is approached as a form of suffering, a therapeutics of the psyche as well as of the body is indicated. We are able to acknowledge and embrace weakness, limits, dependence, and loss. In addition to providing opportunities to both increase the acceptance of suffering and lessen its perceived severity, the progressive shocks of chronic illness can become a means to being a more conscious participant in one's own life.

THE FIRST INITIATION

THE FIRST INITIATION that chronic illness offers is into the world of disease and medicine, a passage marked by bodily ordeals and emotional trials that test our endurance. This initiation resembles traditional ones in several ways. It is not chosen by the initiate—illness befalls its selected participants uninvited. It calls on many rituals and accompaniments also found in traditional initiations in cultures around the world. It includes rites and ceremonies involving masked elders (physicians) with arcane language and knowledge, special lodgings (hospitals, offices, test facilities), body piercings with needles and probes, states of altered consciousness, forms of undressing for the initiate, an overall atmosphere of mystery and foreboding, and an expectation of significant change of role and status.

It may seem that there is almost no end to the procedures that are performed on many of us in the medical quest for proper diagnosis and treatment. To enter the initiation process most of us consult a medical professional. Past experience, level of comfort, cost, and the accessibility of care are important variables that influence when and how we enter into medical settings. Most of us do not first visit a physician because we know we have a disease. We go to a doctor because we don't feel well or we note a significant change in some function.

Our decision to go to a physician depends on the meanings that pain and distress have for us and our families. My occupation, personal history, and cultural attitudes may lead me to accept physical pain and discomfort as a normal part of life, leading me to dismiss the need for medical consultation as long as I can function in the roles I consider important, whereas you may more quickly identify a similar sign as evidence there is something wrong. Or we may seek out a physician when someone else has noticed enough of a change in our behavior or appearance to raise concern.

Often we wait to see whether the change persists or worsens before making a first appointment. We might consult friends and family members to learn if they have had similar occurrences and how they dealt with them. We may turn to the Internet and medical self-help books, of course, and question acquaintances associated in some way with health care. We might be encouraged to try out nontraditional practitioners, who are sometimes helpful. Finally, if symptoms continue, this extensive, often anecdotal, information-gathering process may culminate in a request for an appointment with a doctor.

As we reach for medical care, we may feel as if we have given up control of our physical boundaries, as if we were colonized. In fact, there is no other activity in which our bodies are more examined and explored than modern medicine. A Western physician might perceive a "diseased" body as either a problem to be diagnosed and solved or a beautifully designed machine in need of surgical or chemical repair and cleaning. Other specialists move in with their own views and solutions. Needles violate our skin; blood and a host of other fluids are withdrawn; tubes as well as television cameras (!) are fed down our throats or up our colons; microelectrodes are attached to muscles and nerves. Skulls are drilled, abdomens sutured, and tissue of all kinds is cut, removed, replaced. Anesthesia renders us unconscious, and powerful drugs induce chills, convulsions, fevers, and fatigue.

For some people (like myself), this information gathering process before, during, or after diagnosis can serve as a defensive strategy that we engage in to avoid confronting what we fear might be the truth. Still, we can use the process to develop our ability to sustain the virtues of the patience of not knowing and tolerance for ambiguity, which will serve us well in the years of uncertainty that accompany most chronic illnesses and disabilities.

EVERYTHING DEPENDS ON EVERYTHING ELSE

WE RARELY TRAVEL the road to diagnosis alone. More often than not, others—our family members and friends, additional health care professionals, insurance company employees, and managed care personnel—are involved too. The diagnosis of chronic illness is the outcome of a complex web of interactions among a number of stakeholders, at a minimum, physician and patient. We may not even be present for the majority of discussions that result in a particular diagnosis, making the process even more foreign.

Victims of crimes frequently feel peripheral to what has happened to them after they report the incident. Their experience is taken over, managed, used, or discarded by police, prosecutors, and attorneys in the pursuit and trial of the perpetrator. Victims have a big stake but little say in how the process goes forward or in determining the fate of the guilty. Sometimes, we and our families experience the same traumatizing feelings of helplessness once we enter the medical system. Our descriptions of our illness and our beliefs about its origins are often neglected or abbreviated in favor of a medical account shaped more by the doctor's beliefs and experiences than our own.

Not that the physician's hypothesis of cause or diagnosis is inaccurate—but it is too thin. A richer description would include my and my family's hypotheses as well, for that is where clues to ease the suffering, if not to cure the disease, are likely to be found. The attempt to discover a cause that leads to a treatment that works is also a pursuit of meanings and explanations that cohere and bring some relief. My search for cure or healing may also be a journey to find people willing to test out new hypotheses, or as importantly, to share stories of pain and hope.

The essence of emptiness, according to Buddhist thought, is that everything depends on everything else. And so it is that even after we are placed within one diagnostic group, we may be shifted to another. Legal battles are fought over the financial consequences of the assignment of disease causes and classifications, as we have seen in cases of disease, disability, and death apparently related to tobacco use, drinking, exposure to asbestos, breast implants, and mining. The process can take years and may not be resolved until death and autopsy.

There is another hurdle if we suspect we have (or are identified as having) chronic conditions such as attention deficit disorder, mental illness such as depression, drug and alcohol addictions, Lyme disease, or neurofibromyalgia. We often find ourselves mired in doubt or negotiation among the assorted parties to a diagnosis— patient, family, physician, school, insurer, governmental agencies, corporate and academic investors, and scientists. We may even be told that "No such thing exists."

From these transactions, some of us emerge with a diagnosis of chronic illness. With chronic illness, we struggle to make sense of the collection of symptoms and signs, prognoses and changes that produce our distress. The realities of sickness and care are built by ourselves, our physicians and families, and our culture in the same way that our memories, sensory experiences, and ways of seeing and being in the world are constructed. The interested parties, lay and professional, sick and well, patient and healer, negotiate diagnosis, prognosis, treatment methods and goals, fees, degrees of disability, concerns about compliance, and so forth.

The process affects the outcome: The ease or difficulty of the process influences the illness itself, adding or removing levels of distress. It is often impossible to separate the bodily complaints that result from the underlying pathology of tissue and organ, framed as a disease, from those that arise from the emotions, strains, and social and political context in which the illness experience is first embodied and formed.

This first initiation under the hard hand of illness often leads us to grapple with fundamental questions about life's design and significance. What is happening to me? Why am I suffering? Who am I? What is my life worth? Is my life a good life? What do people in families and communities owe to themselves and each other? How much suffering is too much? Is there any goodness or meaning to be found amid pain and loss? How can I be healed? These are questions with which many of us, and our families, are seized.

MY DIAGNOSIS, 1979–1982

THIS IS HOW I remember it. On a spring day in 1979, I left my car at a local service station for a minor repair. As I walked the three-quarters of a mile home, I noticed that I stumbled as the toe of my left foot seemed to drag behind me and stub itself on the ground. I wondered whether passing drivers or even my neighbors might think me drunk. I let the incident pass and was bothered no more except for an occasional trip on the stairs.

At that time I was a practicing psychologist at a children's hospital, married for eleven years, and the father of two children. Our family owned and participated in a movie theater and its internationally-respected resident stage magic company. One of my roles was to change the metal letters on the theater marquee every weekend night. As the seasons rolled into summer and fall, I experienced more and more difficulty keeping my footing as I hauled the wooden crates full of letters from their storeroom upstairs.

On Sunday show days, costumed as a toy soldier, I stood on a small platform behind a stand and sold souvenir programs. My leg and back would become strained before the curtain was raised and I could get down from my perch. Quickly changing into another costume, I rushed backstage to assist with props and make a brief appearance during one of the magic tricks.

But more and more often, an unexpected urge to urinate could not be denied, and I would run to the bathroom. There were even several times when I wet myself, but I managed to conceal the stain. I spoke of these events to no one. I just carried on, assuming that most of my symptoms were psychological. The tightness around my abdomen, difficulty sleeping through the night, urinary problems, fatigue, paresthesia, irritability—were these not characteristic of anxiety disorders?

On Thanksgiving Day that year, I could no longer carry on as if nothing were wrong. I had been swimming in a warm indoor pool; when I got out of the water my strength was sapped, I could barely stand or walk. (Months later I learned that an early diagnostic test for multiple sclerosis was to place people in warm baths and observe the temperature's effect on their bodies.) A severe back spasm the next day brought me to the hospital and, after reporting my recent symptoms, I was admitted. I entered the hospital for an evaluation to rule out a spinal cord tumor. Two days later, following several evaluative procedures of varying levels of discomfort, I was discharged with a diagnosis of viral lesions of the spinal cord.

I did not know that this was an umbrella label for the cause of my symptoms, which would not be until diagnosed three years later. At the time, it seemed to me that my life remained unchanged. I accepted with apparent unconcern the incidents that once in awhile literally tripped me up. I just chalked them up to the spinal cord lesions and put them out of mind. I had too busy a life to think about what had never occurred to me at all—the possibility that I might, in fact, be ill.

The idea of illness was not remotely in my mind. As a child and young adult I was rarely ill, nor could I recall serious illnesses in my immediate family. Even the death of my grandfather when I was thirteen seemed more an outcome of his old age (seventy-four) than the cancer from which he had suffered.

Three years later, on a blazing hot summer weekend in 1982, my wife, my children (ages eleven and eight) and I climbed down an embankment toward a lake in the White Mountains of New Hampshire. Shockingly, I could not make my way back up the small slope. I had no strength in my legs; my wife Sheila had to support me on her back and arm and drag me to our car. Returning to Massachusetts, I entered the hospital for a second time. I left with a diagnosis of multiple sclerosis.

By Labor Day I was unable to ride a bike or walk for more than fifty yards without collapsing from fatigue, and an assortment of other symptoms had appeared. I had frequent episodes of urinary urgency and occasional incontinence. My wife reminded me—pleaded with me—to go to the bathroom before leaving wherever we happened to be, but I hated the feeling of powerlessness that accompanied the realization that I needed to do such a thing. Consequently, I often neglected to make sure I didn't have to go, and accidents occurred. In one particularly horrific instance that year, I attended a wedding in New Jersey, armed with new medication to increase the holding capacity of my neurogenic bladder. I ate and drank during the festivities without regard to the risk, putting faith in my new prescription.

How relieved I was that the drug worked so effectively—I never had to make my way to the restroom at all! On the way home, however, the dam broke. Through New Jersey, Connecticut, and Massachusetts, I peed and peed, helpless to control the flow. My pants, my socks, my seat, all were soaked, making it impossible from my point of view to make my way to the men's room at a highway stop. Even if I managed to change my clothes, the upholstery was thoroughly drenched; nor did I know whether my bladder had finally emptied.

During the next three years, my life was filled with changes that at the time I did not connect with my diagnosis. After all, I told myself and others, the worst part of my MS was the sadness that unexpectedly caught me on spring days when I saw other people, alone or with companions, riding their bikes along the country roads and seaside ways in our town. The sense of freedom and spontaneity that such sights invited reminded me of my losses, and I attempted to keep my grief from spreading beyond the images in which I contained it. Sheila freely admitted her own fear and pain, but I insisted that I was really not in denial as she suggested.

Yet within the first three years after my diagnosis, I left the magic show and community with which I had been intimately involved since I was twenty-one years old, resigned from the hospital where I had worked for seven years, stopped practicing psychotherapy, took a position as director of the nonprofit Institute for Human Evolution then resigned from that role to start up a magazine for parents, and, when that endeavor was not successful, resumed work as a psychotherapist in collaboration with a neuropsychology practice.

On a winter night in 1985, I placed my Apple IIe on the kitchen table, put a filled teapot on the electric stove, and began to write a book to help individuals, couples, and families cope with the effects of multiple sclerosis. When I next looked up from the monitor, the water in the pot had evaporated and the pot was welded to the cooktop. I wrote with passion and ease of the difficulties, dynamics, and strengths of people with chronic illness, drawing upon the lives of the people with whom I worked in therapy. Yet not even when the manuscript was published was I able to imagine or acknowledge that any of the events of the previous few years were linked to my own experience of, and coming to terms with, my chronic illness.

A PAINFUL DIFFERENCE

A traditional story tells of seven blind men attempting to describe an elephant. One touching the tail dismiss-

es the animal as no more than a rope. Another, his hand upon the leg, says it is a pillar. A third, brushed by its ear, calls it a fan. A fourth, arms outstretched across the body, states definitively, "An elephant is a wall." The next, tapped by the point of the tusk, declares it to be a plow. The sixth man, gripping the trunk, pronounces the beast a great serpent. The fable instructs us on how much our conclusions are based on only a small fraction of total information. And what of the seventh blind man? He is ourselves, presuming that our interpretation of the tale's meaning (for example, the one I just gave) is the true one. So it is with many illnesses whose symptoms present in ways that lead to uncertain and, to some, controversial diagnoses.

CHRONIC ILLNESS IS a change, whether bodily or emotional, that makes a painful difference in the world we take for granted. Chronic illness is, of course, not the same as time-limited illnesses, such as a cold or flu. Maybe a good parallel is the difference between a broken leg and an amputation. Take a farmer from any land or field for millennia past. When he does not return to his farmhouse one afternoon, his wife and son go to find him. He is lying on the ground next to his mule clearly in pain, unable to stand. His leg is oddly bent; very likely it is broken. The farmer will require a board and wrap to hold the fractured bone together to set and some sort of stick to lean on until it is mended. It is possible no one would seek the aid of a healer, bone setter, surgeon, or X-ray technician. And it is very possible that the farmer will be behind the plow in a month or two with no more than a limp and an ache when it rains to remind him of his injury. He—and we—can think of the event as a relatively simple thing.

It was what it was and it passed. We can say the same of a cold, an acute event that passes. Even some heart attacks may not result in a chronic condition. Despite a dangerous event that may result in a dramatic temporary change in wellbeing, the patient may return to a relatively stable *status quo ante*.

But what if the farmer's leg had to be amputated? Or became infected? What seemed at first to be one thing transforms into another. With chronic illness, patients don't "get well." Symptoms continue or progress over a long term, in the crucible of time, and impair our ability to continue with significant activities and normal routines. There are often periods of exacerbation and remission. Frequently, each remission returns us to a lower baseline of functioning. Think of a tennis ball bouncing down the stairs: the ball always bounces, but never as high as the last bounce. Unlike the farmer's broken but not infected leg.

WE DON'T SUFFER FROM DISEASES

A centuries-old tale from ancient Greece, "The Ship of Theseus," suggests a paradox that the ill share with those not yet afflicted, even if the well are not aware of it. Theseus sailed his ship on mythic adventures throughout the Aegean Sea. By the time he returned home, every oar, plank, sail, and line had been worn and replaced. Yet the ship's name remained the same and its old sailors thought of it as the same vessel on which they had seen so many wonders.

PHILOSOPHERS HAVE DEBATED whether the ship is the same despite all the changes it endured. Illness, just like birth, puberty, and indeed, death, is a profound transformation of our being in the world. It is a lesson in the flesh of the notion of nothingness, the delusion of permanence amid the continuity of sameness and change. We may look the same; our environment is the same. Yet everything is different.

The very chronicity of certain illnesses and disabilities makes it likely that unexpected and physically limiting effects as well as many other unanticipated changes will continue to arise over time. It is painful for us to fully face the implications of having the set realities of our everyday life suddenly become unstable. We change as our illness changes, its shape-shifting manifestations calling to mind Heraclitus's dictum, "No one steps in the same river twice," as neither the man nor the river are the same. We don't suffer from diseases, we live our own idiosyncratic experiences of illness.

It is of course important for us to focus on what remains constant amid the multiple changes, cascading losses, endangered meanings, fears, and anxieties that chronic illness may bring. Yet even while still giving comfort and proffering hope, it is essential for all—us and our families—to look straight at the facts on the ground. We need to attend to our illness and how it affects ourselves and the people in our lives from the angle of its world-unmaking capacity. The assault of illness upon me is not simply physical, it is ontological, affecting my very image of myself—my being—my circumstance—my world.

A desk emerging from trees and ending in ash, a disease, a disability, a life—each is a framing of a brief moment. Nothing is permanent. To what passage in time do I become attached and with what consequence? Imagine a diagnosis of chronic illness as the pinning and labeling of a butterfly. Useful, but it tells just a little of what it is to be one, being a caterpillar, metamorphosing, flying, sipping nectar.

Chronic illness is a sped up illustration of our fate, the impermanence of each of our lives. The word comes from the god Chronos, serpentine in shape, whose consort was Ananke, the personification of destiny or fate. They wrapped the primordial cosmic egg and when it split the ordered universe emerged from chaos. We are born, we pass our time, we die. For most of us, until older age settles upon us, we barely notice how briefly we burn.

A World Unmade

In one of the most widely known wisdom stories, a gentleman on a nighttime stroll comes across his friend on hands and knees under a streetlight, obviously searching for something he has lost. The first fellow graciously gets down to help. After a fruitless hour or so, he asks his friend where he was when he noticed he no longer had what he was looking for. "Back there," the searcher said, pointing down his unlit driveway. "Why are we here then?" the gentleman sensibly inquired, to which his friend replied, "The light's better here." Now, this tale most often ends here with a laugh at the seeker's foolishness. But the true story goes on, for the dark was not where he needed to be—the right place to be looking was wherever he was at the moment. "What I need to find," he said, "is me."

DURING THE LONG period between the onset of his symptoms and diagnosis, my friend Tom shared with me that he felt as if he was looking at the world and at himself "through broken glass." "I've felt that way ever since the doctors were concerned enough about my symptoms to ask for more tests," Tom added. "I'm young, I have a lot to look forward to, a lot I want to do. I have played by the rules just like my parents taught me to, and now everything feels like it's going to break. I think it's the belief that my life is supposed to go along a straight road if I live a straight life, that I could take for granted, naive as that sounds, a lot of things. I'd get sick when I got old, not now. I could keep my body in shape with the right food and exercise. That I could plan on things being a certain way in the future if I did certain things now."

As a consequence of his not-yet-diagnosed symptoms and his need for medical treatment, Tom fears he can no longer continue in his current employment. His income is likely to decline, and his wife will probably have to work longer hours in a physically demanding job. As a result, despite his new physical limitations, Tom will have to assume a measure of the care that his wife now provides for their children and his ailing mother-in-law. His concern about his ability to drive safely even now forces him to arrange physician and physical therapy appointments to fit his wife's already crowded schedule.

Tom and his wife spend less time with friends—their social life falling victim to the financial-belt tightening they have undertaken and the increased fatigue they both experience. The leisure activities they enjoyed before, both as individuals and as a couple, required time and fitness, and each now has less of both. There are fewer opportunities for intimacy between Tom and his wife; when they do take place, expressions of anxiety about the present and future predominate.

Although nearby relatives and friends offer emotional and logistical support, Tom is reluctant to accept their help because he does not know how he can reciprocate their kindness. At the same time, he notices what he thinks is a worsening of symptoms. He's reluctant to share his worries and cause even more distress to those he loves. Tom often awakes early in the morning—the time he calls "the hour of the wolf"—and wonders what has and will become of his family and himself. He puts off falling back asleep, fearing that he will awake to one more trouble in a world gone wrong.

I note the ABCX model of family stress theory. "A" stands for the stressor event, "B" for the resources (familial, financial, professional, environmental, etc., available to cope with the stressor event), "C" for how we define the event, what meaning we give it (a chance for everyone to pull together? an expected contingency in life? divine punishment?), and "X" for the degree to which the outcome of the initial event is experienced as overwhelming trauma or as simply a difficult event.

Pileup occurs when multiple crises draw resources from each other, increasing the load on family members, drawing down reserves of energy, time, and morale. The devil is in the details, so pileups are excellent fields for work on our efforts at non-attachment to images and expectations.

THE EXPECTABLE UNEXPECTED

THE DALAI LAMA once suggested that he enjoyed problems because they served as mirrors with which to see himself more clearly. The devil, for Buddha, was the aspect of his own nature that did everything in its power, both subtly and more grossly, to keep the Buddha from attaining enlightenment. Buddha's struggles with his devils in whatever form they appeared were, like all of our challenges, the actual path through which he pursued his aims.

Two months have passed since our new Tibetan Terrier pup, Kai, came to live with us, and it's been everything friends warned us about and all we expected. He has been the kind of teacher that chronic illness can be, but a lot more fun. And at times, Kai, expressing his puppy nature, plays the little devil. We had a picture of how things would go based on our memories of his predecessor, Bodhi. But of course, they are two different (both lovely) dogs, as we are now altered people.

Much of this is characteristic of what happens when one family member has chronic illness and another, often the caretaker, experiences a fall, illness, or a change of job hours or travel. So whether a puppy or an accident, how we respond to the expectable unexpected reveals a great deal of how well we live our lives in the present moment. Do we become impatient with Kai's puppy ways? Do we quarrel with one another? Do we doubt our decisions and question whether we should return Kai? Yes to all of those actions and doubts. And then, as we do with any unexpected shower, we raise our umbrellas or put up a tent, allow the rain to pass, and move along the path we're making and taking, with unseen difficulties and beautiful vistas waiting around unmapped twists and turns and with Kai by our side.

EVERYDAY LIFE

As Gregor Samsa awoke one morning from uneasy dreams he found himself transformed in his bed into a gigantic insect. He was lying on his hard, as it were armor-plated, back and when he lifted his head a little he could see his dome like brown belly divided into stiff arched segments on top of which the bed quilt could hardly stay in place and was about to slide off completely. His numerous legs, which were pitifully thin compared to the rest of his bulk, waved helplessly before his eyes.

What has happened to me? he thought. It was no dream… What about sleeping a little longer and forgetting all this nonsense, he thought, but it could not be done, for he was accustomed to sleep on his right side and in his present condition he could not turn himself over. However violently he forced himself toward his right side he always rolled onto his back again. He tried it at least a hundred times, shutting his eyes to keep from seeing his struggling legs, and only desisted when he began to feel in his side a faint dull ache he had never felt before.

—Franz Kafka, The Metamorphosis

ILLNESS ASSAULTS THE world of our everyday life, a world we inhabit without much conscious thought. The largely unexamined presumptions of what our world "is" and how it "works" enable us to get on with our business in that world. Its features, knit together into a routine way of taking action and making meaning, make up much of the fabric of our lives. It is through this world that one initially experiences illness, and it is the coherence of this world that illness most directly threatens. Thus starting with a firm grip on the features of everyday life will give us a better handle on the shifting terrain of illness. The world of daily life is largely one of meaning. Meanings help us connect one thing with another. We recognize patterns amid clutter.

It is difficult to accept what we perceive as betrayals by our bodies. Yet, acknowledging the new role and rule of the body is the first step toward maintaining composure and keeping mishaps from turning into calamities. Apprehension about fainting, enduring a convulsion, or suffering nausea or dizziness in public is surely an understandable reason for those of us with chronic conditions to restrict our activities to places where we are sure of some privacy, comfort, or relief. Many of us with illness train ourselves to inhabit a range of territory we know we can comfortably manage, restrict the type and amount of food we eat or drink, and limit the time and energy we spend in any activity or encounter. We manage lives of "normal" agoraphobia.

We are guided through this new landscape by an assortment of bodily habits and dispositions, mental images, internal voices, and emotions. Each acts in and upon the others, shaping and reshaping personal and larger social, cultural, and environmental realities. In the world of dreams or delirium no other person needs to exist, but neither a person nor the world has much meaning apart from the other. There is no question that rocks can exist in a world without people, but their meaning, if it could be said to exist at all, would be entirely different. But the notion of a person without a world is difficult to imagine. Each of us inhabits a life-world that is in some ways identical to that of all others. In other ways it is similar to that of our shared groups—tribe, community, family, profession, gender, and others. Finally, our own unique and distinct portion is defined by our biographies, genes, bodies, and personal store and stock of interactions with the worlds of others. As we act in and upon the world, the world, in its turn, influences and impresses itself upon us.

Of course, most of us are conceived in the childhood fantasies of our parents-to-be as far back as their preschool years, as well as in our parents' intimate discussions long before the physical acts that initiate the biological development that culminates in our birth. We exist as a consequence of the most basic of interactions and continue to need and be transformed by them. Our mother's gaze, how we are touched, the immersion in the "simple sea of sound" of our parents' lives directed toward us or around us all influence not only how we will grow, but whether we will thrive or live at all.

As fundamental as we believe our own bodies to be to our own being, they exist only because of our interactions with the bodies of others. It is impossible to imagine a self coming into being without relationships. There are literary speculations and legends about children reared by wolves or in isolation. Of course, they do not develop as individuals or social beings. Charles Cooley's notion of the "looking glass self" suggests that our self-image is a product less of who we actually are than of how we rightly or wrongly believe others see us. And we put a great deal of effort into managing the impressions we wish others to have of us.

The general molding of our senses and bodies to keep unacceptable impulses and, eventually, thoughts at bay becomes our "character armor." Over time the winnowing out of a repertoire of acceptable postures and gestures, thoughts and words, inevitably leads to a complex and tightly woven fabric of habitual movement and familiar and intimate sensation that we characterize as "me" or "I." Eventually we justify the bias of our normal by rationalizations. Because we are creatures who want to make sense of what we experience, we give ourselves "reasonable reasons" for the feelings we have and actions we take toward ourselves and others. Our sense of normal literally derives from the habitual stance we take toward the world, the posture and gestures and even thoughts that feel comfortable to us, that seem right.

THE "I" BECOMES ONE THING, OUR BODIES ANOTHER

THE ABILITY TO manage what, when, and where material goes into and comes out of our bodies is one of the earliest goals of the process of socialization. As toddlers, we are praised for demonstrating control of bladder and bowel, as well as for spitting, burping, coughing, and holding our own spoon, fork, or cup. Most parents show concern when these competencies seem to be delayed. Children who wet their pants or beds feel shame. The pee and poop jokes five- and six-year-olds tell show the anxieties many feel about their still-recent achievement of such a potent symbol of social maturity. It is a mark of personal mastery among some of us not to give in to the promptings of nature when "more important" matters are at hand. In those worlds, our duty comes before our "doody."

At the other end of life, even though we view the loss of these capacities for body regulation among the elderly as a sure sign of aging, a normal and somewhat inevitable prelude to dying, many older persons are afraid as well as discomforted if they have accidents because they may precipitate more restricted lives or institutional care.

As we grow up, our bodies disappear from consciousness. They are rendered secondary in our attention to other, more important concerns. Gradually, the experience of a place (usually in our heads, in our culture) that we each call "I" becomes more dominant. In most of our elementary schools, for example, movement of the body is seen as disruptive to learning and a source of distraction. The frequency of recess is reduced and a physically active child is viewed as a classroom problem. Increasing control of the body is seen as a mark of maturity. Thinking becomes identified with our brains and the remarkable intelligence of the moving infant and toddler is defined as a stage to be left behind as thought becomes more abstract.

The "I" becomes one thing, our bodies another. The figure of the ego establishes its commanding relationship to the ground of our bodies, just as a general directs strategy, expecting his troops to carry it out without knowing the individuals under his command. Prior to illness, the body becomes an instrument in service to its presumed master's aims. The body overthrown is thus the unconscious, a living embodiment of possibilities unexpressed, a source of less socialized and potentially creative imagery, movements, and intuitions.

With the onset and progression of chronic illness or disability, the relationship between our bodies and the "I" is altered. The person who has no signs or symptoms of the tumor that grows treacherously and unknown deep inside his brain neither experiences nor construes himself as ill, despite the threat the growth poses to his existence. But when symptoms appear, his formerly absent body becomes present in a way that his ego does not intend. His attention is yanked away from the "I-witness" world of everyday life to the body-focused world of illness and pain. It is this change in the gestalt of consciousness and being-in-the-world that is central to the experience of illness.

Prior to illness, our body usually stayed out of consciousness unless we chose to bring it onstage for acts of pleasure or while mastering new skills. In the background, it stays quietly at the ready, like a servant in a PBS British period drama—capable, unseen, unheard. Riding a bike to work, enjoying sex, tossing a football with your daughter or son, relishing the sensory favors of intoxicants, putting eye and ear in the service of paintings and music, are all occasions when we want to take some notice of how our bodies move, respond, and quicken.

We each assume our body is able to perform the routine actions of everyday life. In a fluid suite of actions that require little or no conscious attention, for example, I turn the ignition key, engage the gears, press the accelerator pedal, and drive off. I talk and walk, carry a cup of hot tea with no fear of tripping, falling, or spilling. I type, focused on finding the right word without giving my fingers the least thought. I read, engrossed in the plot and rarely concerned about the neuro-physiology and biomechanics of vision.

These well-practiced ensembles of movement and meaning—"kinetic melodies," in the pioneering neurologist A. R. Luria's phrase—are built up over time through ordinary use and intentional practice. Our bodies are always with us. Awake or sleeping, well or ill, in infancy or old age, during puberty or pregnancy, the ultimate fact that "I" am embodied never goes away. But because we have our bodies, we are alive, lusty, and *limited*. We depend on the environment and others, and are subject to the certainties of aging, loss, and death.

Bound as we are within our bodies, suffering indignities and experiencing joys, we can still enter with empathy into ways and possibilities of being that exist beyond our own. The gravity of our illnesses is shaped by what our bodies mean to us and how and for what we purpose we use them, as much as by the clinical symptoms they present. Just as our bodies are affected by how we think and feel about ourselves, our identities are similarly influenced by how we experience our bodies in a circular and self-reinforcing manner.

Thus the illusions of our selves are spun, as in the tale of The Emperor's New Clothes.

> *There once was a vain and foolish king who prided himself on his fine appearance, his taste, and his wisdom, each of which he notably lacked. As they passed through a neighboring kingdom, two clever tailors heard of the foolish ruler and thought of the gold they might spin out of his delusions. Admitted to the royal chambers, the two tailors proposed to the king that they sew for him the most fabulous wardrobe of color and cut and cloth extraordinary. And only those as discerning and wise as the king would be able to see his finery. He rapidly accepted the cunning tailors' offer.*
>
> *We know the end of the story. The king's pride kept him from admitting he saw nothing at all of the supposedly unsurpassed clothes. And it was only during a royal procession when a child called out among the stunned subjects, "Hey, the emperor's got no clothes!" that the foolish monarch saw his naked being beneath his cloak of vanity and pride.*

The role of the child who declares the truth of the emperor's delusion and nakedness is embodied by our illness. Fixed by no rules, disrespectful of authority and limits, it does what it pleases. We are never quite sure how our bodies may present themselves from one day to the next. We are possessed by shape-shifters, beings of indeterminate appearance who make the familiar strange and the strange familiar. When our bodies become ends of concern in themselves rather than a means toward other ends, we probably have moved from everyday life to the world of illness.

The child/ fool is a familiar figure in literature and legend. Perhaps the image of the under-socialized, misshapen fool who is the one who speaks dangerous truth to power is an apt way of explaining how the pathology of chronic illness and disability can undermine the grand fantasy of normality. Often portrayed as a dwarf, deformed and limping, dressed in motley with cap and bells, the fool is a figure of derision and scorn. But he shadows the king. With wit and riddle, he alone speaks truth to power.

In some cultures, there are figures of ambiguous sexuality, cloaked in animal skins who interact in different ways with the gods. Perhaps the fool descends from the shaman, the powerful healers of another age. The laughter the fool gives or gets tempers the tensions of court and king. Illness and disability curb the ego's hunger for dominion. The common pathology of the wearer of crowns reminds us of the necessity for limits and the humility of the person at the social bottom.

THE TEXTURE OF TIME

FOR INDIVIDUALS AND families living with chronic illness, the experience of the present is likely to acquire a texture much different from what prevailed before diagnosis. Illness disrupts the large and small tides and rhythms that we hold onto in the flux of our lives. Lifelong patterns of sleeping, waking, eating, and defecating are often disturbed. This is no minor matter. Mood and emotions, fatigue and morale are closely linked to the assurance of the regular satisfaction of our most basic needs.

Interrogation, torture, or periods of battle or natural disaster that interrupt, threaten, or deprive individuals of their accustomed sched-ules often produce powerful and lasting effects. Indeed, as patients have long complained, strict hospital routines of waking, feeding, and temper-ature-taking can produce, even if unintentionally, states of passivity, agitation, disorientation, and dependency.

The structure of time within which our fami-lies live may be rendered uninhabitable by chronic illness. No longer does the expected follow the anticipated, as it did before illness arrived on the scene. And when the rhythms of our lives are altered, the very nature of our existence can become problematic. The "I" of "Who am I?" is no longer the same. The activities during which time passed quickly and through which aspects of our identities were affirmed—a favorite hobby, work, the play of sex, cooking for a party—now take "forever," or pass too quickly if they are enjoyed at all.

I might see and fear my body getting worse, and now I have more time to think about it. There are fewer places where I can go, because it takes me longer to get ready, to get there, and to get around. Many of us have goals and plans, and we are proud of that fact. Perhaps we feel we are not just guys who did stuff on the spur of the moment. We do things that make sense in terms of what we want to accomplish for our families and ourselves. But without those goals, or at least the possibility of reaching them, some of us may not be sure who we are or who we are supposed to be.

Those of us with illness are not the only ones who suffer from the twisting of time. Those with whom we share our lives are often disrupted as well. Family members of all ages may be called upon to rise to the occasion or to take on certain roles before (or sometimes after) they ordinarily would have been expected to.

Most of us take for granted a normal progression of the life cycle. We expect that increasing accomplishments and engagements in the world will gradually give way, over some seventy or eighty years, to lessening involvement with its desires and demands and a coming to terms with death. But as a consequence of illness, the timelines for meeting the challenges or confronting the crises that characterize personal, family, and cultural stages and cycles of all kinds are frequently extended, compromised, neglected, or seen as completely unattainable.

We may not think about the patterns of time in which we live until we get sick. It may then seem that we have both more and less time. It takes us more time to get simple things done, and we feel like we probably have less time to do what we really care about, because this illness is progressive. And one hell of a nuisance. We wake up when everyone else is sleeping, and we're just so exhausted when the rest of the family is ready to go.

The time frame in which we live is wrenched out of shape. What is included on the canvas of the present changes. The future may lap at the margin of the next twenty-four hours, or even closer, whereas before illness brushed our life it could extend out some months or even years away.

The attempt to live "one day at a time" serves different motives and different functions as illness and circumstances change. For some, it can be a defense against ongoing discomfort or a style of coping that momentarily relieves suffering. At other times, it may help deflect thoughts about anticipated losses or inspire people to focus on using the present moment as richly as possible. For one person, "I take it one day at a time" is a proud announcement. For someone else, it is a weary sigh of resignation. And as I meditate each day, I may notice that both thoughts are present and called my own.

LIFE IS SUFFERING

"LIFE IS SUFFERING," the Buddha stated as the first of the Four Noble Truths. The Pāli word he used for suffering, *dukkha*, has its roots in the term for a cart's axle badly fitted to a misaligned axle hole. The ride in such a cart is bumpy. The longer the trip, the greater the possibility of breakdowns, damage, and discomfort. Whatever the cart owner's plans, much can go badly. Perhaps the Buddha saw such a cart on his first forbidden excursion beyond his father's palace walls. In English, the word *suffering* has its roots in the Latin *sufferer*, derived from the Greek *pherein*, to bear or carry a heavy weight. Let's imagine, then, that to suffer is to carry the burden of having a damaged cart or body.

Wise men and women suggest that some degree of suffering is unavoidable. But they also distinguish between kinds of suffering: necessary or unnecessary, conscious or unconscious, inevitable as with aging or brought on as a consequence of indulgence or greed, sudden and acute or enduring and feeding on its own misery, intimate or insistent on infecting others.

Much of our suffering, as underlined by the second Noble Truth, is a result of our attachment to our desires, not simply of our desire itself. Do we suffer because we desire food or shelter or to be good? Surely, it is more than desire itself that causes suffering. I, for example, desire some ice cream. Unfortunately, we have none. Okay. I'm fine with that. It is what it is and life goes on. Or do I jump up and down in frustrated rage? More likely, due to my attachment to my desire and feeling a lack of fulfillment, a dissatisfaction will emerge: life cannot be good or worthwhile if I can't have my ice cream. And it will gnaw.

Of course, it is natural to want good health. Being human, we experience disappointment or sadness at its loss. But we can learn to limit the amount of unnecessary suffering caused by false beliefs about our illness—for example, our belief in the necessity of the absence of illness to live well, or our mistaken identification of our unfulfilled desire for bodily health with the totality of our being.

A second type of suffering is the grief or sadness that naturally arises from death, injury, or loss of those we love. This is an emotion built into our human nature. To survive as children, it is fundamental to seek attachments to and bonds with specific others. The absence of these feelings may indicate a defect in character, not spiritual achievement. These emotions inhibited the Prince Arjuna, as described in the *Bhagavad Gita*, from going to battle against his relatives, dear friends, and honored teachers. Krishna, charioteer and divine advisor, did not dismiss the legitimacy of Arjuna's emotions, but engaged in dialogue with him about how best to practice the detachment necessary to perform his duties as adult warrior and prince despite them.

On the other hand, there may be a "too much-ness" to the natural, even inevitable mourning of such loss, as when a mother or father ignores the well being of living children because of the death or illness of another child. The gods were offend-ed by Achilles's enraged grief over the death of his beloved Patroclus, that was fueled by Achil-les's shame that Patroclus was killed on the battlefield while he sulked in his tent, his honor insulted, disrespected by the war king Agamem-non.

Physicians face this painful dilemma as well. The best do not want to numb themselves to the suffering of their patients. They wish to be able to give hope and at the same time to acknowledge reality. They want both professional detachment and human feeling.

We can be doctors for our own souls. It is not

possible to memorialize the sufferings of each of us or of our families. Maybe it is useful to approach loss from a variety of angles, reminding us how far, wide, and deep the damage may spread. Like the waters of a flood, illness can penetrate everywhere, leaving little untouched and rendering much unrecoverable. How is it possible, we may ask as the toll mounts, that our lives can in any way recover?

The experience of loss, after all, is at the core of being human. Gods take what they want from mortals and then leave us—abandoned, broken, sometimes ecstatic, always changed. Asked who his masters were, Freud answered, "The Greek tragedies." We often forget that Oedipus's story was one of abandonment and exile from beginning to end.

The meetings of god and man are often followed by separation. In the Christian faith, God is broken in a most terrible way and followers are bereft. The Bible is filled with stories of war and loss, Israelites are enslaved, children slaughtered by the angel of the Lord. The anticipation and reality of loss is bred in our bones.

"We have to find ways to handle the experience of perpetually grieving, of never being out of grief," commented one psychotherapist who works with HIV groups. Perhaps those who live with or alongside life-threatening illness are not so different from others, for all of us are surrounded by sorrow whether we are conscious of it or not. Are many of the signs of physical distress characterized as illness—somatization, anxiety, depression—expressions of that sorrow? Is illness itself a form of grieving?

WE FLEE FROM SADNESS

A king of old, bereft by the loss of his beloved daughter, raged against his fate and the ceaseless tears that streamed down his face. He fled from his sadness by leading his armies in savage conquest of other lands. When this did not eliminate his grief, he turned to his ministers, physicians, and wizards to locate for him, under penalty of death for failure, a sorrow-ending potion or charm. Many died before a small child presented the king with a roughly carved ring, inscribed on the inside, "this too shall pass." With that, the king's madness found peace.

WE OFTEN DEFLECT attempts to discuss sad topics, unable, apparently, to tolerate loss and distress. Families with illness sometimes shield children and intimates from the sadness that is a common partner of loss. Some of us do not wish to express sadness around our children, fearing we will harm their trust and faith in a safe or good world.

As parents, we may believe that children who know grief or danger will suffer unnecessarily. Sadness, from this point of view, is a trauma to be avoided. How often is a child who expresses sadness met with the simple, quiet acceptance of a parental hug? Too often, we point out why the child need not feel so sad, or we propose a plan of action so that sadness won't happen again. Often, with divorce, for example, one parent attempts to speak no ill of the other, regardless of their behavior, leaving children confused as to why any divorce took place or either parent is upset or angry. A child may learn to not trust their own perceptions or to be wary of the truthfulness of others.

It can be easier to devise strategies to cope with guilt than to simply sit still with sadness. I see many people in grief who tell me that their mourning was compounded by friends' and families' desires, communicated in more or less subtle ways, for them to move on. In our culture, the work of mourning is attempted through a vocabulary of affects—anxiety, depression, angst, stress, and the like—that locate the source of anguish in our individual body or mind rather than in the community, environment, or trans-cendent order in which we also live. What is there about the mourning process that seems so essential? How can it be used to facilitate the healing of those of us and our families who are touched by illness?

The work of so many painters, musicians, writers, and other artists flourishes in spite of—possibly owing to—their physical afflictions and other experiences of loss and grieving. Why would this not also be true of those who are less artistically gifted? Are not richer relationships, accomplishments in the face of great odds, experiences of joy and humor, battles for social justice, taking a stand for one's own dignity, and the simple satisfaction of making it through the day also creative possibilities that we may realize as a sort of pentimento of grief?

There are dangers implicit in our concept and worship of health. Inevitably, the messiness and pain of illness erupt into the sunlit clarity of the taken-for-grantedness of daily life like a ragged man at a politician's ball. In some ways, couldn't illness be helpful in our culture? Illness is one of the few remaining humble and personal forces to oppose the powerful social ideals of health, adaptation, and productivity. Without illness as a grave reminder, our personal and social fantasies of mastery and wealth might recognize no limit.

Religious, spiritual, and archetypal meanings are among the few resources that we may seek when serious illness enters our lives. Even if we don't consider ourselves to be religious or spiritual, these realms can inform us in matters ranging from the meaning and cause of illness, suffering, and death to specific religious practices. It is possible that a sense of the sacred and of fundamental good has at least as significant an impact on many of our lives as parents and family do.

Modernization and its accompanying attitudes have undercut the plausibility of religious beliefs for many, but they have not removed the sources of distress that elicit them. Human beings continue to be stricken by death, illness, poverty, war. Unfortunately, we lack the stories, mythologies, and beliefs that made these facts of life easier to bear. We no longer live as if the wounded healers such as Gilgamesh, Jesus, or Moses are alive among or above us.

From a traditional religious perspective, illness and death are symptoms that reflect humanity's continued fall from a pre-Eden golden age. Physical suffering is an outward display and reminder of the distress and the distance from perfection and wholeness that all humans share. The sight of a physically ill person ought to evoke the wish to harbor, comfort, and heal. Our communal failure to do so, whether as a result of inadequate insurance, weak support programs, fear, or any other reason, demonstrates from a spiritual orientation that we are all ill. The religious attitude is important, because it calls us to witness and care for the suffering other as we wish to be healed ourselves.

DEFENSE MECHANISMS

Plato uses the allegory of the cave to describe the depths of illusion and fear that keep individuals clinging to their ignorance of reality. A group of people are chained in the cave facing inward toward its wall. Behind them is a fire. In front of them, but behind a curtain, other people go back and forth carrying sticks with objects upon them that cast shadows upon the wall.

The prisoners mistake those moving images as reality. Even when a prisoner is forced into the world outside the cave, he resists opening his eyes. When he finally does, he slowly sees and accepts the sunlit reality he perceives as superior to the shadows of the cave. Upon his return to the cave, now blinded by the darkness as before he was by the sun, his fellow prisoners take his closed eyes as evidence of the danger of the world outside the cave and vow to never leave the dark ignorance they safely inhabit.

D EFENSE MECHANISMS ARE among the most useful aspects of our way of being in the world. They can also be, literally, the most dangerous. Many of us are familiar with a few terms as a result of our own self observation, Psych 101, or the popular language of AA which all describe denial, rationalization, intellectualization, and regression.

Regression is a reversion to earlier forms of

behavior (putting my hands over my ears to avoid hearing bad news). Intellectualization is a focus on the analysis of a situation rather than its emotional components (when I was first diagnosed with MS, I would describe its causation [demyelination], historical origins [medieval Europe], or symptoms, but not its actual current or potential effects upon my life). Rationalization is familiar to all of us because we employ it so frequently, giving ourselves plausible but false reasons for what we say or do ("I can't go to that event because of the weather," when actually I'm lazy or self-centered).

And there is denial. Probably the psychological buffer most widely known in recent years because of its association with AA, and the alleged inability of alcoholics to acknowledge their addiction. But it's applicable elsewhere. I engaged in denial when I did not get automobile hand controls early in my illness, despite putting myself and others in danger every time I drove.

In most psychological texts, defense mechanisms are presented as unconscious means by which we protect our self-image, pride, or vanity from perceived threats to their ability to sustain themselves. We rationalize self-centered acts, for example, because we firmly believe ourselves to be caring.

But let me go beyond that. What is so dangerous that it is worthwhile to lie about it or not to see reality clearly? I suggest that what these mechanisms actually defend against are attacks on two fundamental beliefs at the core of our modern notion of an autonomous and integrated self.

First, we want to maintain the experience of ourselves as individuals. If we were "undefended," we might see how often what we do contradicts what we say or how we see ourselves in our mental mirrors, and that can be a shattering experience. The person we think we are might turn out to be but multiple fragments of a non-coherent individual. No one, but many. The "I" is no self, but a construct, a named label that holds our ever-changing modern body and mind together.

Secondly, without these defenses that hold "me" in place, I would *feel too deeply*. Defenses resist life encroaching upon my fixed pictures and firmly held beliefs. Observing my contradictions, my selfishness, my pettiness, my ignorance, I would feel so deeply ashamed. Conscience would awaken. These mechanisms keep us from feeling in our bones the fundamental facts of life—we have bodies that will age and sicken and die over time and we also possess a spirit that in its limited time can be truthful, compassionate, alive. Defense mechanisms are a spell that keeps us enthralled to the demon of ignorance.

John Newton, the composer of "Amazing

Grace," wrote his hymn after he survived a storm while captain of a slave ship, fulfilling a promise he made to the Lord if he were saved. With illness, frailty, and dependence we, too, are blessed with a great need to be honest with ourselves. The alternative is enslavement by the true illness and disability of self-deceit and delusion.

Denial and False Pride

"For the good that I would I do not: but the evil which I would not, that I do."

—Romans 7:19

I was reluctant twenty years ago to try the first medication I was prescribed for MS, and I stopped after a couple of weeks because I didn't like the side effects. I put off using a recommended cane, delayed moving to a walker, and didn't consider a wheelchair until a nurse predicted an earlier death from injury, hospitalization, and skin breakdown and infection if I avoided one. These are small examples of the all-important issue of denial and compliance. What is the use of treatments unless we use them?

There are many reasons we don't comply with medical advice. Fear is a common one. The refusal of some parents for their children to receive vaccinations for smallpox in eighteenth-century England, for measles in twenty-first-century America, and polio in Afghanistan are examples of non-compliance based on fear.

Denial is particularly damaging and selfish, because it affects family and friends, not simply oneself. Continued smoking or drinking after a diagnosis of tissue damage, not following through on dietary instructions for diabetic or heart conditions, or not drinking enough water despite a history of urinary tract infections are common examples of non-compliance based on, perhaps, denial or a wish to assert one's autonomy against the social, medical, or parental "should."

Drinking water is a particular problem for me. For years I had problems of urinary incontinence and urgency. I trained myself to minimize water intake before going out, limited carbonated beverages, and did other things that I'd read astronauts do while awaiting take off. But once I began self-catheterizing about fifteen years ago, I no longer needed to limit water. In fact, the opposite was necessary. I've had a very difficult time training myself out of the old habit I spent years building. There's still a small voice that warns me against drinking too much water and calculates time for bathroom breaks. This week a friend told me he'd read that using a straw increases the amount we drink. I got straw; so far, so good. I'm not asking why, just retraining myself to be slightly more compliant.

Not complying can give some of us a sense of control. Our diagnosis of chronic illness or disability usually marks the beginning of a lifetime of great uncertainty. At least, as my body changes and my treatment is so often in the hands of others, I can say no to *this* regimen, prescription, or recommendation.

And then there is our attachment to self and to body images of ourselves. For a long time, I put off using a walker because I didn't want to be an old guy shuffling around with yellow tennis balls attached to my device. Somehow I completely ignored my actual body holding myself up with a cane on weakened legs. I looked like an upside down L.

Finally, our great deluder—false pride. In fact, I could easily say that at least four of the deadly sins—pride, gluttony, wrath, and sloth—play a role in our refusal to do what is in our best interest, or continuing what is not. And I'm sure we could make a case for the others—greed, lust, envy—as well.

Let me add, of course, the requirement that what is recommended is sound and we have done our due diligence, whether through our experience with a trusted physician over the years or second opinions or other trustworthy sources. Our willingness to follow up or comply with the treatment recommendations of medical professionals is highly variable. The likelihood that those of us for whom treatment does not offer immediate relief, or whose illness is not directly life-threatening, will go along with suggested regimens is actually quite low. But if the cost and side effects of prescribed medication are minimal, the chances of its continued use are much better than if expense and discomfort are present.

For most people, the social, time, financial, energy, and other costs of pursuing recovery or delaying progression are weighed against an assessment of likely outcomes. We make perhaps uninformed cost-benefit analyses: A short-term high cost of compliance is different from a long-term high cost, just as a low probability of benefit over the short term does not necessarily predict low benefit over the long term. We and our families also often think differently about medical situations involving an elderly person than those involving a child.

We must fit compliance with medical advice into the jigsaws of our lives. I know from my experience and from talking with others that exercise or physical therapy are unlikely to be pursued if financial strain, transportation, child care, or other logistical barriers get in the way. Illness does not exist in a social vacuum. All of us, whether afflicted by illness or acting as caregivers, have multiple roles, and our role related to sickness is one among many.

Finally, I know that much of my noncompliance is an oppositional expression of my wish to be consulted and heard, or needing time to get used to the idea of a procedure or intervention. And how often do physicians or therapists check in to see whether their recommendations are being followed or if help is needed? It is, of course, finally and fundamentally, a delusional assertion of life without illness!

Guilt

It is not uncommon for a well partner to feel guilty for remaining able-bodied while the other partner is ill. Sometimes the efforts of caring that the well partner undertakes—so exhausting that they may seem "beyond the call of duty or love"—may represent a wish to undo feelings of betrayal caused by failing to protect the loved one from suffering and hardship.

It is important to understand that there are seldom single or simple motivations for thoughts, feelings, and actions, particularly in circumstances as complex and difficult as illness and disability. We have to recognize that although our feelings of guilt for another's illness are normal, we are in no way responsible for the illness. Often, despite frantic efforts to maintain our lives as they were before, it is painful for us to acknowledge that our lifestyle is different and will be different, and that there is little we can do to maintain our prior status. In fact, our current actions might prevent us from making necessary adjustments.

Here is where we must find the difference between lifestyle and life values. Our style of living might change, but our values need not alter. In fact, illness or disability may force us to reconsider what is most important—career, children, marriage. We have to think about that seriously. We need to reflect upon this, for if we are not clear about those choices, as soon as things get rough one or both of us might be angry or confused.

Simply feeling guilty does not necessarily mean we have done anything wrong. It may also be that we are experiencing *existential guilt*, the experience of a normal person when people they care for, known or unknown, suffer distress. We cannot take care of everybody in need, but feel we should. It is a part of the non-psychopathic essential goodness of humans. Unfortunately, we do not have unlimited resources. We cannot be at all places at all times. We cannot do it for those at home and we cannot do it for those we care for, stranger or friend, far away. We do what we can do, and it is natural and good to feel guilty about that which we cannot do, no matter how much we wish otherwise.

PRACTICE MAKES…

PERFECTIONISM OUGHT TO be one of the first "shoulds" we give up as we experience the jumbles, fumbles, and tumbles of chronic illness and disability. Can we do anything right? Are there plans that do not go awry? Once ill or disabled or aging, even the most simple acts we did perfectly well, from tying shoes to holding forks to walking, can turn into a series of un-forced errors and mishaps. And this does not include the more complex tasks at work or at home, including sports and relationships, that can cause us to become harshly self-critical when we are not able to perform them "perfectly." It is quite arrogant or delusional to imagine perfection is within the realm of the humanly possible.

After all, God created the heaven and earth, the animals, Adam and Eve in six days, pro-nounced it "good"—not perfect, but good—and on the seventh day, he rested. Immediately, there were problems: Adam and Eve, Cain and Abel, the flood. Oy! If God himself needs to promise, with the sign of the rainbow, that he will not destroy all humans because of his frustration with the imperfect beings he created, how can we presume to get angry at ourselves for our imperfectly lived lives?

David Winnicott, the great British pediatrician and psychoanalyst, introduced many concepts we still value today. "Good enough parenting," "transitional object," and "holding environment" are all terms he introduced into the culture of child rearing and that find applicability in all of our lives whether with children or not. The good enough parent is one who provides the child with "optimal frustration," that is, experiences with limits. When the child reacts with tears, anger, or collapse, the mature parent does not rage, walk away, or give in. She calmly holds the line. Better the child gets practice in a world that often does not deliver what he wants in the secure and ultimately forgiving arms of a parent than all of a sudden confront a far less benign world unprepared and unpracticed.

Illness gives us a chance to be good enough parents to ourselves, to face our many limits, some unexpected and others too familiar, without rage, collapse, or abandoned ambitions. We can meet our falls and failures with equanimity and grace. We are going to get a lot of practice at imperfection.

A saying commonly associated with the Jesuits, taken from *The Imitation of Christ* by the German cleric Thomas à Kempis, is "Man proposes, God disposes." Many of us add "God willing" when we propose a future action or outcome. "Not my will, but thine be done." All these phrases suggest limits on our ability to influence events. It is so universal an acknowledgement in traditional teaching that we may give it the status of a law as firm as Newton's. In fact, George Gurdjieff gives it a name, "Second, or denying, force."

We make a plan, to drink more water, for example. Immediately all kinds of events, ranging from external distractions to internal moods or preoccupations, "conspire" to foil our efforts. We are probably much better off when we suggest to ourselves, and when we evaluate others who provide us with care and comfort, that "Practice makes better, not perfect."

SLOTH

MONKS AND FOLLOWERS in most spiritual traditions are warned against the fault of laziness lest it lead to the greater fault of what is called in Christian writings *acedia*, one of the seven deadly sins. Acedia, sometimes called sloth, is a state of indifference either to the outcome of one's practice or to the efforts required to achieve one's meditative or prayerful aims. Kathleen Norris describes it as "not-caring, or being unable to care, and ultimately, being unable to care that you can't care."

In ordinary life, sloth may lead to lack of discipline, shoddy work, and ultimately to poverty and its harmful effects on family and community. Although acedia can be associated with depression, it is not necessarily. For example, distractions of entertainment, gambling, cell phone use, and other "sinful" pleasures, excessive daydreaming, even too much "idle time" in the library, or discouragement about rewards for one's efforts could be signs of sloth.

Most importantly, acedia, as is the case with many other "sinful" acts, is one of "wrong" thinking, for it is the thought about the perceived object—not the object itself—that leads us astray down the crooked path. I fall into this trap when I blame a newspaper article about a person with MS who is "better" or "worse" off than me for "making me" despondent or fearful, rather than taking responsibility for my own thoughts and not allowing them to lead me "into temptation."

The reason I bring it up is my own struggle with sloth. After all, I make the effort to use my illness and disability as a means to greater mindfulness and "work" on my being. However, falls from bad transfers and the need to call EMTs for a lift assist have greatly diminished—hopefully even been eliminated—with the recent installation of an overhead sling-less lift that takes me from bed to wheelchair and back. I do have to pay attention so I don't get whacked in the head with it, but the need to carefully focus is admittedly less.

Then, of course, there's the mechanical wheelchair that has all but replaced my manual one. The manual chair built my strength and endurance. Now, unless the weather lets me outside in my wheelchair bike, I have to remember, like any other sedentary guy, to lift my two-pound weights. Unfortunately, as we all know, it is very difficult to remember to remember. And when I do, the usual excuses we all share chatter away in my mind. For example, right now I'm in writing flow and don't want to interrupt it and exercise.

I am grateful for the greater safety the lift provides to my caregivers and myself, and for the increased comfort and mobility of the new chair. But part of my challenge now is to prevent the lessening (surely temporary) of some difficulties from lulling me to sleep, causing me to miss the obstacles and make the most of the opportunities to wakening we all share. I'm sure in the near future I'll look back at this essay and wonder whatever was I thinking, and be grateful for this brief period of a little ease.

For some of us, the experience of chronic illness is one of total catastrophe, akin to losing our worlds. The losses and suffering are so overwhelming that more than our identities are at risk. The self or "I" that is able to reflect upon or construct a life story or narrative faces obliteration. In response to the question, "Who are you?" we might answer, "I am nothing, worthless, without hope."

Pain—sheer, awful physical pain—can leave no room for a new story to be told or an old one reworked. Paralysis also can so dominate the field of being that the afflicted body cannot yield to the play of imagination and conceive a future despite immobility. The inability to fulfill our roles as spouses, fathers or mothers, lovers or friends can lead to feelings of shame so powerful that no self can survive.

Suicide is often disparaged in our culture. In other ages and traditions, however, the ability to choose one's own death when the goods of life are destroyed has been a mark of virtue rather than a fault. With no expectation of cure, we may live with few needs and believe that we makes minimal claims on others. We are content to see the skull beneath the skin. The intimations of our own mortality give us, we believe, greater insight into the valley and shadow of limits and death in which we all walk. In a world of transient pleasures and questionable goods, we may choose to bear our suffering with the "patience of Job."

Our sense of irony can be quite magnificent, but can lead to a sense of superiority over less "enlightened" souls. The detachment we have achieved by wanting very little enables us to be kind to others who are struggling for health or success.

Our illness complaints are not expressed through verbal insults against body, physicians, or fate, but by an unwillingness to move beyond our self-imposed boundaries of possibility and motion. Labeling us as "depressed" not only is wrong, it discredits our world and what it offers us. The melancholic soul of Ecclesiastes, for example, judges the worth of the things of the world better than most others do.

SCHADENFREUDE

A WONDERFUL WORD that names an emotion that is poorly regarded in every tradition is *schaden-freude*. To my ear, it sounds onomatopoeic, a gentle hush with a chilling twist at the end, like an assassin's blade. Schadenfreude can be most simply defined as taking pleasure in the misfortune of others—or, "I'm glad it's not me!"—and, more broadly, envy at others' good fortune. (Another terrific phrase with much the same meaning is *morose delectation*, the compulsive enjoyment of an evil thought, as if running one's tongue over a broken tooth. But I'll stick with schadenfreude.)

The relevance of schadenfreude to those of us with chronic illness and disability is considerable.

There may be times, after all, when we are jealous of what others can do that we cannot—take vacations, for example—or be able to meet friends in places that are not handicap-friendly, or make arrangements in a fraction of the time we need to plan.

We may act out by being critical of our friends' destinations or reluctant to hear their tales. What's the big deal, we may say to ourselves, imagining that we see our little world in greater depth, proud that we have such a small carbon footprint compared to the mileage others put on in their sky-polluting flights.

Of course, the motivation behind the thought is less environmental concern and more a passive aggressive jealousy for their particular good time out of our reach. We also might harbor a secret smile that the weather was not as warm as they had anticipated. Surely, if asked and after a moment of self-reflection, we would not wish our friends bad luck, but there are occasions enough when we may have a quick flash of thanks that they, not we, are victims of ill fortune.

It is no different than the reluctance we may feel at visiting another couple or family who seems happier, healthier, better off in some way than our own. At times we direct this feeling toward ourselves rather than others and feel depressed or self-critical. In the early years of my illness when I could not bike or walk longer distances, I did not enjoy sunny weekends. I preferred clouds or rain, huddled in a corner with unconscious self-pity. An excerpt from one of my earliest related poems, "Exacerbation," expresses a bit of what I felt.

> I'll admit it. I was scared, dragged back
> to the early days when humbled by illness,
> I envied the doings of the careless,
> confident striders
> among the well, the healthy Houdinis
> unshackled by time
> who swiveled on bikes with a kid's ease
> counting circles of knee and wheel to race
> home.

In Catholic tradition, to sin against the Holy Spirit is a most grievous, unforgivable fault. As I explored this idea that I had always vaguely associated with schadenfreude, I learned that it initially referred to envy of a companion's spiritual progress. How many "spiritual" communities, churches, fellowships are not filled with this? As is true with so much of what takes place in ourselves, there is a tension between the animals we are and the humans we wish to be.

How apt that neurological studies show that strong feelings of envy stimulate physical pain nodes and reward areas are turned on by learning that the envied have suffered misfortune. In fact, brain imaging reveals a significant correlation between envy and schadenfreude. With these brain mechanisms in play, I suggest that it is possible to be addicted to schadenfreude.

Clearly schadenfreude drives us away from other people. For some of us it is harder, for others easier, to avoid being ensnared by envy, gloating, or the self-indulgence of unnecessary comparison with another's life. Krishnamurti spoke frequently about how ill-served we are by comparison with others. In addition to not truly knowing their lives and struggles, "If I am always comparing myself . . . what has happened to me— what have I done? I only compare in order to gain, in order to achieve, in order to become—but when I don't compare I am beginning to understand what I am. Beginning to understand what I am is far more fascinating, far more interesting; it goes beyond all this stupid comparison."

From a Buddhist perspective, one of the ten meritorious deeds is to rejoice in the worthy accomplishments of others. Indeed, I have learned there is a word, *compersion*, for feeling pleasure in others' pleasure. We can even become enthusiastic for our well or able-bodied friends; that is *entheos*, filled with the spirit of God and good. I am so glad for you! And that is not a bad thought to have.

THE LIMIT OF OUR BEING

"EARTH'S CRAMMED WITH heaven and every common bush afire with God." These words of Elizabeth Browning are painted above the archway of the room where we eat, overlooking the flower strewn yard where I now sit in my wheelchair next to a sleeping Kai, my mind constantly distracted from the focused tasks of reading and writing by the breeze grazing my hair, the sound of whispering leaves, distant lawnmowers, and bird song.

My undeserved bounty humbles me. Any complaints I may have about my lot I acknowledge as truly petty and privileged, first-world chronic illness bits of unnecessary whining, irritability, or impatience.

On the other hand, the poor man, crippled by pain as he propels his simple wheeled board along a crowded city street, hoping for enough beggared coins to help his family get by for another few days, is an obvious and deserving recipient of compassion and generosity.

But in the face of life's true facts, we are equals. Both born to live and to die, to laugh, to cry, to sing, and to sigh. Each of us then has the same possibilities of using our life circumstances to be and to breathe. I use these extremes simply to make the point that the differences in the situations of one or another reader of these thoughts are not likely to be as great as we imagine.

A favorite phrase of mine, first used by Freud a century ago, is "the narcissism of small differences." He observed that friends, peers, and fellow members of social groups are fundamentally very similar. We highlight the slightest ways we differ from each other to accentuate our specialness, often ignoring the possibly greater ways we are not like some others. One example might be how some German Jews thought themselves superior to Shtetl Jews, though all eventually suffered the same fate. Another is the social ranking that some African Americans formerly gave each other based on skin color. And, of course, there is the undeniable privilege afforded many of us by levels of skin pigmentation.

Who am I to be bummed out for more than a moment that I have an illness and you do not? The philosopher Gurdjieff suggested that when we are overwhelmed by inner or outer suffering, or we have lost the thread of attention and presence, we have reached "the limit of our being."

What being is that, I often wondered. It is, I think, human being. Lost in daydream or comparison, envy or pride, pleasure or tears, the difference between me and Kai or a tree or a boulder is very small indeed.

COILS OF THE SERPENT OF DESPAIR

WHEN ILL, WE are often caught in a continually winding spiral of suffering, or *samsara* in Sanskrit which means *circling*. I am reminded of the magic circles or repetitive tasks from childhood tales in which the victim, as a result of being diverted by some enticement while on a mission, is ensnared by a witch's curse, goblin's trick, or day dreaming mind.

The circles are not literal ones, yet they tell us of something quite real. They speak of the contingencies of existence. The cycling of fear/denial/fear. When the black crows of anger or disbelief at my situation peck away at me or the rats of fear gnaw at the heart of an ill friend, I know we are in the thrall of neurotic delusion. Neuroses are recurring thoughts and behaviors that provide short term pleasure or pain avoidance, but at the cost of long term negative consequences. We get endlessly that which we seek to avoid.

In my case and perhaps yours, the imprisoning circles are the obsessive thoughts that surround our worsening illnesses. Is this an exacerbation? A new infection? Will it require an increase of care or is it a stage toward further disability?

The circle also symbolizes the compulsive acts we repetitively employ in our attempts to avoid the limits and inevitable fates we encounter as mortal humans. Perhaps going from doctor to doctor. Trying alternative systems of healing. Eating differently. Loading up on this or that supplement, nutrient, or vitamin.

We get caught up in these mazes of doubt and confusion when we forget about the great destroyer, time. Any one difference or change in treatment may improve health for the short term, but eventually you, I, all of us will find no relief from our common end.

How often we forget about the subjectivity of time, and how dependent our experience is on the way it is measured and lived. A second, minute, hour, day, month, or year for us can be matched against the number of breaths or heartbeats before we die. Indeed, if I have a pulse of 75 beats per minute and I live to 85, my heart will beat 3,350,700,000 times! (Is that correct? Check my math.) And we worry that one day it shall, it must give out?

Yes, we may fear how short or brief our lives are. But a beat, a breath, a life for most other creatures is even shorter. What is a day to a moth, a dog, a monkey? And it is true our duration is a flicker compared to a sequoia, a planet, a star.

Our beliefs and pictures of how life ought to be are fixed upon an unconscious fantasy of an eternity in Eden. And what kind of life would that be? As my friend François says, "You can replace everything, man. You can replace your car, your house, even your wife, but you cannot replace what you have now—your life. This is it, man! Live!" And let us loosen the coils of the serpent of despair with attentive presence of mind on the path that leads us out of the circle.

THE SECOND INITIATION

WHEN THE CALL COMES

The Minotaur, half man, half beast, is contained within a maze to protect himself as well as others from his frustration and rage at his mixed condition and conflicted nature. Theseus rescues Ariadne from the maze by following the thread she holds to the center of the Minotaur's world. We too need threads to help lead us out from the constrictions, turnings, and unsatisfied hungers we experience along the labyrinthine paths of our illness and disability.

FOR MOSES, JONAH, Paul, the call to awaken to greater consciousness came through a voice. But sometimes we are summoned in silence, as when we find ourselves in a situation that confronts us with choices or challenges we never expected, from illness to accident to violence. So perhaps illness is a visit from the gods, who leave behind a mystery of value unknown—danger? a gift? a new capacity for love? death? a summons to listen for meaning?

Illness confronts us head on with a marvelous paradox: the reality of impermanence—all things must pass, nothing stays the same—juxtaposed with the truth that we have to go on living, continuing to desire a full and richer life. Religions, spiritual traditions, cultures, philosophers, teachers and each of us in our own way, consciously or not, have proposed solutions or acted out ways of living that enable us to exist with dignity, love, and meaning in our time on earth.

I think it likely that spiritual traditions and practices developed in response to the hard and short lives most people passed through until quite recent times. Injury and accident, battle and war, pestilence and plague, famine and drought—the list of perils goes on. Gilgamesh, the Homeric epics, and other early myths and tales sing of physical travail and lives cut brutally, but not unusually, short. Achilles chose a heroic, but brief, life. Ulysses lived much longer, but none of his shipmates survived and their endings did not shine with glory. I'm sure the wisest men asked their questions or received their revelations in full expectation of a life short by our standards, and, to our eyes, filled with physical disease, disfigurement, and harm. Such was the old normal.

A physician's diagnosis can lead us to ask, "How do I connect the fact that I am ill with how I choose to live my life?" Most traditions celebrate virtues such as patience, honesty, moderation, and self-examination. It is interesting to consider how many of these values are consistent with the recognition of limits, imperfection, and humility and have little to do with progress, individuality, or health. To move from being fixed on a cure for the body to being open to the healing of the person and the soul is a profound shift. Might illness be not only *not* an impediment to a good life, but a means toward it?

Many individuals and families absorb the shocks of illness with resourcefulness and resilience. The ongoing and increasing demands of illness overwhelm others, who undergo ever-greater suffering and despair. And there are those who knit together well-made lives out of the threads that fate has spun. For them, the illness experience, while admittedly difficult and painful, is a source of significant meaning and spiritual worth as well. My MS, diagnosed almost forty years ago, is not cured. Yet my path toward healing and making a richer life from the stuff of suffering continues.

Illnesses challenge our confidence, pride, and belief in determining our life course. Fortunately, understanding liminality—the ambiguity of transitions—and working with it constructively may well provide an opportunity for these afflictions to open a door to the second initiation, one toward greater consciousness. Indeed, as a result of a "crisis of consciousness" that is triggered by symptoms and diagnosis, the functions of traditional initiation rites are activated that may reveal new layers of meaning to existence and its spiritual dimensions. They push us to face the reality of death, and potentially liberate new sources of energy by shaking up habitual bodily structures and patterns of movement.

Chronic illness, serving the purposes of traditional initiation rituals, helps us learn to endure suffering. Central to the initiatory experience is a process of unmasking and disenchantment. The spells of taken-for-granted meanings and assumptions about our everyday lives may be broken, providing us with greater freedom to choose our conscious values. The challenge to or loss of identity and bedrock beliefs based on previously internalized values is a natural, although at times terrifying, process in a human life.

The second initiation, *possible but not ensured*, takes place through our conscious use of the illness experience itself. We can no longer live as before, taking our world as it is with little thought. Our attitudes toward suffering, our bodies, and time are challenged. And, of course, an illness does not affect just ourselves alone. For better or for worse, our relationships with family, friends, and community are altered. Unexpected moral and ethical issues may arise for all.

After all, most religions or traditions encourage compassionate relationships to others, urge gratitude for the gift of life, call on us to wake up and enjoy our brief existence, invite us to serve something greater than our wants and needs. In sum, it is my claim that physical limits are consistent with the goals and means of spiritual paths, that we can choose to use our afflictions as a way of transformation toward more conscious way of being in the world, and moreover, disabling or chronic symptoms can have a generative effect on our creative possibilities.

CRISIS OF CONSCIOUSNESS

In many wisdom tales, a disciple is given very specific instructions. When she completes her task, the teacher insists such a mission was never assigned or that the student completely misunderstood what she was asked to do or that she took words too literally. Whichever way she turns or however she tries to do the job rightly, the disciple is confronted with her alleged inadequacy. She inevitably misses the point. Like the fool in the tarot, she is at the edge of a cliff, the dog of desire nipping at her heels, paralyzed by her thirst for knowledge, unable to go forward, her fate forbidding her to step back.

Only when the seeker gives up her usual approach to problem solving, or recognizes the futility of reason, or gets that sometimes there is no "solution" to the most basic facts of life's limits, can she be free of the need to search. She is shocked by the stone wall of her teacher into realizing not only her ego's weakness

*faced with the unpredictable force of nature and her
own pride, but the arbitrariness of conventional
norms and social institutions as well. The master
wants to evoke a crisis of consciousness in the student
to disrupt the automatism of thought and feeling with
which she passes through her taken-for-granted world.
So it is with the inescapable facts of life and chronic
illness.*

THE IDEOLOGIES OF progress, individuality, and
health are among those that strongly affect our
attitudes toward illness. Modern society's
elimination of many social and medical ills lends
much credence to the argument for progress.
Most of us assume that human culture, over the
long run, is improving, as demonstrated by the
feats of technology, science, and the power of
rational thought.

We easily forget that the concept of human
progress is recent. Not more than three hundred
years ago, and in traditional and fundamentalist
cultures today, human history was imagined as a
fall from an original state of grace, or a descent
from a once-upon-a-time golden age. In this view,
the evolution of humanity is inconceivable except
as a result of divine intervention. Individuals may
take steps along a path toward perfection, but any
success they experience typically occurs in spite
of, rather than because of, the existing social
order. So difficult is the real evolution of being
and consciousness, according to some traditions,

that its attainment is possible only after many lifetimes of effort.

"For every problem, there is a solution," is a belief so familiar that it is a cliché. The facile endings of so many television shows and the barrage of advertising for goods that promise to fulfill so many desires or remedy so many ills reinforce this message, as many critics have noted. Our unquestioned commitment to the ideologies of progress and health contributes to the drive of many physicians to leave no treatment stone unturned or intervention untried.

We, too, are often willing to undergo whatever miseries the attempted cure may bring. I believe it is an unexamined and unwarranted attachment to a belief in progress and a problem-solving orientation, as much as a hope for recovery, that keeps many of us with chronic illness and our families searching for a cure despite disappointments. The grip that these taken-for-granted ideologies have on us also adds to the anger we may feel toward our physicians and other care providers when our conditions do not improve. From this angle, the experience of chronic illness seems remarkably similar to the conditions for spiritual teaching developed in various traditions.

TAKING RESPONSIBILITY

A STEP TOWARD the second initiation is to take responsibility for my illness. What do I mean by this? Did I cause my illness? It is possible, but very unlikely. Chronic illness is something that happens for a variety of causes, known and unknown. There is no blame. Most illnesses are multifactorial in their causation. Genetics often play a large role, as does environment. Is there any evidence that attitudes of optimism or pessimism affect conditions like cancer? Actually, very little. Is there any evidence that particular attitudes are more or less likely to result in cure? Actually, very little.

Then what is taking responsibility? It is simply the ability to *respond* with attention and care in an ongoing way to whatever the fates have delivered to me. Who else but me? One way or another, consciously or not, I will establish a relationship with my illness. Unwanted as it may be, it is a lifelong partner for better or for worse, in sickness and in health.

Yet we may fear that not struggling is surrendering. Some may suggest to us, for example, that we do battle with an illness to overcome it. I may be encouraged to see the illness as an enemy within my body, an alien attacker. Alternatively, we may be told that living as if the disability does not exist is the best policy.

Both of these approaches are flawed. The first creates an unnecessary antagonism between different aspects of oneself. The second denies the reality of both the disease and the human capacity for healing. Unfortunately, to view disease as an enemy or to ignore its presence does not make it disappear. I must get to know it, live with it, come to terms with it.

This doesn't mean that the illness is my friend. Rather, I must accept it as an unwelcome companion on a long journey and acquaint myself with its moods, departures, and returns. Keep a wary eye on it; know when to rest, to push, to struggle, and to compromise. And unlike with a friend, rejoice at its retreats and regret its arrivals. Nevertheless, I should be attentive. I should be respectful. I should be kind.

I also ought to pay some attention and consideration to the words of others when they point out that I may be doing things that make my condition better or worse. At the same time, I shall be wary of where my information or the suggestions come from. I am responsible for deciding which foods I eat—water, plant, or animal. And perhaps most importantly, the food of impressions—what sort of sensory impressions and ideas I open myself to and reflect upon.

The etymology of *responsibility* or *responsible* is quite interesting. The word is rooted in old French back to Latin to *turn toward* and *hear* and *hear again*. In most societies and religious traditions there is an age of responsibility, ranging from early to late adolescence, when one is seen as able and expected to perform religious or social duties. So there is something to the idea that one is responsible if one has heard several times the call to awaken or obey.

There is no question that the day-to-day struggle to cope with chronic illness can be exhausting. We might often despair that the course of the illness can ever be stilled or any losses of strength or function regained. The attempt to stay even—physically, mentally, or emotionally—with a chronic disease may seem noble to us, yet it can be so futile.

What my illness means to me is central to the making and remaking of my illness experience. I realize that I am neither all-powerful nor helpless to cope with my illness. I can live so that my illness effects but does not control my life. I am responsible for defining and choosing how I wish to live within the boundaries that sooner or later we all will face.

Does what is happening to me offer some positive possibilities or am I completely defeated by its presence? Is it a catastrophe that drastically limits my life possibilities? Or does it open up alternative ways of being and doing? Is it a door through which I discover or refresh for myself how to be more present, and as a result what seemed constricting opens upon a broader vista? It is possible to foster attitudes and take actions that make living with chronic illness easier and may in the long run influence its progression and outcomes. In a middle way between struggle and surrender, we recognize that a disease or disability is neither a judgment upon us nor a punishment.

CREATING A NEW GEOGRAPHY

THE CHANGES WROUGHT by illness to our habitual movements and sensations affect, of course, not only the emotions we experience but the manner of their expression as well. If I am in a wheelchair, it is difficult to stomp off in rage or to get away quickly to cool off. Many of the symptoms of a variety of chronic illnesses include physiologic responses that in our culture we have learned to read as signs of emotional upset or stress. Headaches, diarrhea, skin rashes, and fatigue, for example, are all popularly associated with feeling upset.

Many of us use these symptoms as clues: we track them back to their source in some personal difficulty or concern. When we're ill we may come to identify such somatic complaints as manifestations of illness. Often, we have to create a new geography through which feelings are located and alternative routes by which emotions are tracked and articulated.

Oddly enough, if we acquaint ourselves with the worlds of deaf persons or watch ourselves and others closely, we can discover how much we take for granted the web of connections and interweaving of body, thought, emotion, communication, and sociability that we inhabit. We all have personal patterns of posture and gesture, intonation and facial expression. Reflect on how quickly our partners can pick up who we are speaking to on the phone.

What many people without illness cannot understand is how the changes in our bodies affect the way we feel and, in turn, who we feel we are. Feeling the smile on our faces, hearing ourselves laugh, and gesturing with our hands all contribute to our experience of pleasure, our idea of ourselves as happy sorts of persons. Jumping, yelling, or swinging our arms are all things we do because we feel good doing it, and it is also a way of signaling how we feel to others.

Let's say our illness affects our strength, stamina, or breathing. Maybe we get breathless easily. It's very scary. So we're very careful about how happy or excited we get. Being demonstrative becomes more difficult and it's harder to show warmth. We become more irritable. The back-and-forth of feeling and action that we were accustomed to is disrupted and we're disturbed because of it. My body doesn't feel like me, and so I don't feel like me either. I'm a stranger to my body, and I'm not sure there is a "me" that's not my body too.

I think it possible that much of what is diagnosed as depression among chronically ill people is a function of a shift, whether dramatic or subtle, in the body's emotional communications process. Work in the area of trauma has demonstrated that catastrophic events have major effects on a wide array of cognitive, emotional, and physical functions. Postures and gestures are all means by which we express ourselves, ways we show ourselves and others that we exist. The changes in postures and gestures resulting from illness, accident, imprisonment, or other unwelcome events must surely have great impact on my sense of body and, therefore, of self.

As our conditions worsen, it is possible we no longer speak as fluently a "silent language" in the expression of emotions or ideas too elusive for ordinary conversation, for the back and forth between movement and thought may have been disrupted. Remember that our bodies and our thoughts influence and shape each other, thus we and our families must learn to be more mindful of the "silent language" that our ill bodies speak.

WHOLLY BREATH

It is said that after taking leave of his palace Buddha spent many years on the road, following numerous practices, both alone and as a member of various groups. Disappointed with his efforts to awaken from his suffering, he simply sat beneath a tree and vowed to remain there until he attained enlightenment. But how? Then he remembered one day as a child when, bored at a palace festival, he sat down under a tree and found paying curious attention to his own breathing more involving than what went on around him.

He had never repeated the experience, but he also never forgot it. Frustrated by his fruitless search, he repeated that long-ago childhood experiment. And the act of attending to his own breathing, surprisingly, as he continued sitting for several days, became the means to Nirvana. He recommended it to others and its practice became the foundation of all his teaching.

LEARNING, OR RATHER unlearning, how we breathe is perhaps the most important treatment we can provide for ourselves, whether physically ill or not. Why? Obviously, all mammals are born breathing. And how? The diaphragm is a muscle beneath our lungs; when it contracts and moves downward, our chest cavity enlarges and our lungs expand. The air pressure in our lungs is then lower than the air pressure outside. To equalize the pressure, air enters our nostrils or mouth, without any effort or work on our part.

When the diaphragm then expands or relaxes,

our lungs become smaller, the air pressure increases in the smaller volume, and we exhale to equalize the pressure. Diaphragmatic breathing is the breathing we are all born with because physically it is the most efficient. It requires little effort and provides more oxygen. All benefit, no cost.

Perhaps such effortlessness required to simply *be* is the sound of one hand clapping or the face of our mother before we are born? Buddha sat and Buddha breathed. Less of learning, more of unlearning. We never see great singers pulling their bellies in and raising their shoulders to draw in more air. They all use their diaphragmatic muscles, some in very sophisticated ways, as the great soprano Joan Sutherland coached Pavarotti to maximize the volume of air to sing with and to minimize the energy required to do so.

When most of us were children, however, the way we breathe changed. Perhaps we were exposed to atmospheres of anger or fear and we pulled our breath in. Macho and sexy postures emphasize thin or flat waists. We gradually learn to stand at-tension, stomach in, chest out. We take smaller, higher breaths—the breathing of anxiety. We say we breathe through our mouths or noses, rather than in the "hara," the Japanese word for the point a hair's width below the navel.

When we breathe diaphragmatically, on the other hand, we are more easily calm, peaceful, relaxed. Is it possible that when Jesus says to turn the other cheek he speaks not of being hit on the other side of the head, but of a movement of consciousness built on a foundation of right breathing, a movement from threat-based reaction to slower, more conscious choice? Diaphragmatic breathing is the foundation of meditation and mindfulness, the ark that protects us when we are flooded with worry or distress. Certainly there is little doubt that the word *respiration* shares roots with the word for spirit, the divine breath that gave life to Adam. In fact, some commentators suggest that the correct translation for the Aramaic words "Holy Spirit" is "holy breath."

Diaphragmatic breathing is of enormous help to me and many others with chronic illness. By paying attention to the calming breath it is possible to not simply endure, but to lessen discomfort, pain, and worry. It draws attention from the monkey mind running around in our skulls, downward to slow and sure-stepping elephant mind.

I've not had a headache since 1975 when I was a substitute teacher for one day at Marblehead High School. I say that not to brag, but as an opening to discuss some of the realities of facing and living with suffering, primarily physical pain.

I am not someone who thinks it's particularly virtuous to undergo pain if it can be avoided. I don't think "natural childbirth" is necessarily more "natural" than labor and birth aided by drugs or potions as long as the baby is not compromised. I would not be surprised if women in non-Christian (who do not bear Eve's curse) and pre-modern societies were happy to ingest whatever they could to minimize their pain. And truthfully, if I am having dental work close to nerves, I'll happily have Novocain. For surgical operations, let me shake the anesthesiologist's hand.

Yes, I've experienced other kinds of physical pain, some associated with the neurological damage of multiple sclerosis and some with the accidents and grind of daily living. But for most of it, I manage without the need for any pain medication. A good example occurred several years ago when I had an infection in my finger. I needed to have the wound lanced. I was offered a topical anesthetic, but I had a painting class scheduled following the procedure. Due to MS, it was already difficult enough for me to grasp a brush and that day my finger would be bandaged too. I asked the physician whether I would be able to paint that afternoon and he unwittingly paraphrased "Mr. Tambourine Man": "Your hand won't feel to grip."

I told him I would manage the pain myself. I relaxed and he began to cut. The pain, of course, was present, but I did my best to accept it and not enter internal commentary about its severity. I kept my body relaxed, noticing where and when I would tense, and focused on my breathing. The only difficulty was a nurse who kept inquiring if I was okay. I insisted she be quiet and I'd be fine.

My calm and the bearable pain were, I think, largely due to my conscious use of several principles applicable to daily living. First, of course, I relaxed my body using diaphragmatic breathing. I did not resist the pain of the cutting, but was present with it. When we are fearful, our muscles tighten and that increases pain. I also know pain is influenced by personal, family, and social history. It is, to some degree, dependent on the situation in which it occurs. For example, soldiers report less pain than civilians with similar injuries because they find greater meaning, perhaps from the cause or solidarity with fellow combatants and their sacrifice. Knowing this allowed me to put the pain to one side. Another reason I tolerated the scalpel was that I expected a brief procedure, similar to quite uncomfortable diagnostics and interventions I've undergone. Also, I looked forward to painting later that day, a greater good than relieving my pain with medication.

Few traditional paths toward consciousness suggest that we ought not to suffer, but we can learn to minimize unconscious or unnecessary suffering. Physical pain is part of living, as Adam and Eve are told in Genesis. But, as my example points out, what amplifies our suffering is not the experience of pain or even the wish to be free of it, but the attachment to that wish. There are simple ways of modifying much moderate pain that we might otherwise find intolerable. And certainly there are yogis and practitioners who seek to be free of pain through special techniques and traditions. Before spending a great deal of time and energy searching them out, it is useful to remember this teaching story.

> *Two friends are walking along a river bank when they see a third man cross over to the other side by walking upon the water. One is so amazed by this display of what he believes is spiritual power that the very next day he leaves his old life to find a guru to teach him such a feat. Twenty years later, the friend who did not follow the guru, strolling along the river bank as before, sees his old companion striding across the river and exclaims, "How are you, my dear friend?"*
>
> *"Oh, great friend of my youth, see what I have accomplished after so many years of study with my master. Abandon all and come with me to meet him."*
>
> *Apparently deep in thought considering this offer, he continues strolling with his dear friend. They come to a footbridge that takes them across the river. "Ah, my dear one, I cannot accept your kind offer. What you attained after twenty years, I accomplished in five minutes by walking on this bridge."*

So, yes, sometimes for my aches, I just take Tylenol. And I remember the moment many years ago, similarly beneath a tree, when mindful breathing gave me a gift, not Buddha's for sure, but my own, small and precious, and it is with me still.

THINGS THAT GO BUMP IN THE NIGHT

BEFORE WE EVEN know what might or might not go astray, many of us experience our situations as catastrophic, even though significant people continue to be in our lives as before and nothing has yet changed except our fear that our world that might have been, could have been, should have been, can no longer be. And yet we do not know that. We are fearful of the unseen bears in the unknown forest.

When we are consumed by fear, we are probably better off imagining the road ahead, illness or not, as a *journey*—the term originally meant the distance one could travel in one day. We could also remind ourselves of Lao-tse's dictum, "The journey of a thousand miles begins with one step." And we could take one further step and imagine what lies ahead less as "serious" (meaning heavy and grave) and more as "a series," from which the Sanskrit word *sutra* comes, one bead after another on a string. For that is, in fact, the only way we can live, one step, one breath, one bead after another.

Despite our fears of what may lie ahead, we have a choice of how to use the power of our imagination. For thousands of years, seekers in all traditions and faiths have understood that what we picture or hear in our mind's eye and ear has the ability to generate bodily responses consistent with those images. It is true of picturing our partner's nude body, hearing ghost stories around a campfire, or reading news stories of horrific crimes or natural disasters. Whether with lust, terror, or empathy, we often respond as if the event were happening right now to us. That is why in some teachings imagination is *kundalini*, the serpent power that travels the spinal cord linking organs or *chakras* from genitals to brain. It must be treated carefully, handled with respect. Fear is kundalini as the unconscious master of ourselves, the victory of the snake.

> *Orthodox monks used to strengthen themselves against being carried away by unwanted thoughts by visualizing a crossroad leading east to one village, west to another. The easternmost had small, nicely painted homes spaced along dry roads with well-tended gardens and contented beasts grazing in lush pastures. The homes of the western village were ill-kempt with leaky roofs and set in weed choked lots. Paths were muddy, animals irritable with the lack of good feed and care. The monks were to see, smell, travel to these villages as spiritual exercises.*
>
> *When at a crossroads of his daily spiritual work, confronted by fear or desire or unsure of the right*

course of action, a monk was to recall as vividly as possible these village scenes, knowing what train of thought or action was likely to lead him to the village he knew to be the better. There is an immediacy and power in selected images to defend against those generated by fear. Like against like, "spiritual homeopathy," if you will.

If it is used to increase interest in and compassion for the lives of others unknown to us, the capacity for moral imagination is wonderful. In some traditions, the attachment of my identity to an object, whether of the imagination or the senses, is called a form of "identification." I have reduced the whole of my being to a passing fragment of desire, confused my being with a temporary "I." I have traded gold for lead.

Anxiety about the unknown future, whether before or after diagnosis is to be expected, but we would do well to limit it. All too often, for example, we are told what a diagnosis should or will mean for us—in terms of treatment, disability, changes in lifestyle. But who is to say?

A farmer was blessed with healthy sons and beautiful daughters, fertile land and bountiful crops. Admired by his neighbors for his current and future prosperity, he responds humbly, "We shall see."

A gang of robbers raids the village, quickly plundering the farmer whose wealth is visible to their rapacious eyes. Consoled by the villagers for his terrible reversal of fortune, the now near impoverished man calmly replies, "We shall see."

Five harvests pass and the raiders return, natural-ly heading first to the farm where they previously had looted so thoroughly. Now its reduced state is not worth their time or trouble and, mad with frustrated greed, they mercilessly pillaged the surrounding farms. When his neighbors arrive to exclaim how lucky he was to avoid their devastation, he says truth-fully with heart open to his fellows' pain, "We shall see."

TURN THE OTHER CHEEK

MUCH OF OUR suffering is unnecessary. Maybe we have met with a doctor and we are frustrated, perhaps even angry. He has spent too little time with us or she has given us inadequate infor-mation. Whatever the reason might be, we go off dissatisfied. We carry our complaint for several days, repeating the story to our friends and to ourselves, newly aggrieved each time. And our listeners reinforce our sense of rightful indigna-tion.

Unfortunately, we forget that each time we get agitated we are reacting to an event that is no longer present. When we recall again and again some wrong done to us, we harm ourselves with resentment (from the French, *ressentiment*, or re-feeling). The injury results from our reacting to something not, or no longer, taking place, as if it were happening in the present. That might be one definition of delusion. Our past memory is similar to our worries about an imaginary future. Both are examples of resentment, adrenalized re-feeling. Both are types of suffering, both unnecessary.

> *Take the story of two monks newly arrived at a river. A pregnant woman is waiting on the bank, in need of assistance to cross. The younger man reminds the much respected elder brother that they are not to touch even the cloak of a woman. The elder solemnly rejects the rule and proceeds to offer his strong arms to the young lady and carries her across. The younger monk cannot believe his eyes.*
>
> *After putting the woman down on the opposite shore, the monks go on their way, the younger brother shaking his head and muttering to himself. Nearing the end of their journey, he finally turns to his old friend and asks, "How could you have broken your vows?" "My friend," replies the elder monk. "I put her down miles ago while you still carry her."*

The younger monk's initial reaction is understandable, but his continued obsession with his fellow's deed is a self-inflicted wound. So it is with many of our emotional reactions. If we simply acknowledge our first responses to unexpected events—anger or anxiety, for example—and then put them down, that is what it is. We are human, and some degree of reactivity is to be expected.

But when we turn it over in our minds, getting

angry again and again, especially when no constructive action is the result, then we are left with adrenaline ashes. "And unto him that smiteth thee on the one cheek offer also the other," Jesus preached in the Sermon on the Mount. Or, more colloquially, "Turn the other cheek."

This mantra suggests to shift one's consciousness from a reactive state to one of calm, presence, and choice—the being of the elder brother, both at the moment he picked up the woman and when he responded to his younger companion.

There are several things we can do at those moments to facilitate one response rather than another. Of course, the more we practice before events occur, the greater the probability that we can be mindful during these difficult moments. The foundation of all emotional management is to breathe diaphragmatically. A second practice is to remember the transience of all things. It is sad and true that our lives are brief and, no matter what we do, we will pass. With that perspective, how much is a particular situation worth being upset about?

A third effort is to remind ourselves that we actually know little of the circumstances of the person with whom we are upset. We are likely blind to whatever pain she is in or what he was thinking that led to his behavior. What *do* we know of ourselves? Imagine how much less we know of another. Again recalling Jesus' words, "And why behold thou the mote that is in thy brother's eye, but consider not the beam that is in thine own eye?" Remember how little control we have of our own state and, therefore, be wary of judging another.

Fourth, recite a prayer such as Psalm 23, or lyrics from "Amazing Grace" or Dylan's "My Back Pages," or write your own reminder of the peace of unknowing. Finally, and importantly, imagine the fact and energy of our suffering doing some good in some way for ourselves, others, and the world.

A Slip of Mind

I recall one summer day four or five years ago. A group of world-class professional cliff divers were in Boston leaping into the harbor from a museum's cool granite ledge. They fell, arrows of graceful flesh piercing the black sea 90 feet below, leaving behind only a brief feather of water.

Just the day before, in a new van rolling along a New Hampshire country road, we came to a bend where hills ranged in the distance, thick with summer greens, and I wept for the freshness of the view. The next morning, after reading about the divers in the paper, I was transferring from my wheelchair to the stair lift while day-dreaming about my excursion the previous day. I mixed up my legs, right foot on the wrong side, and slipped a slow two feet from seat to floor. I can't afford to lose myself with a body that cannot function without an attentive mind to serve it.

As odd and grandiose as the comparison may be, it seems to me that the wheelchair transfer has something in common with the divers' feats. Both require full preparation and attention and then a leap. A bad fall on my part, in fact, might have consequences as grave as an error by a diver.

Of course, being mindful, as with meditation, is as much about noticing our lack of attention when, in retrospect, we failed to pay attention, as it is about a sharp-eyed focus on the here and now. Our attempts at mindfulness are supported by precisely the things that are likely to drag our attention away. For illness, like life, is not a concept but *stuff*—a button, pebbles, thoughts, fever, frustrations . . .

Take the apparently simple routine of putting on pants. I have to somewhat consciously string together many bits and pieces of action and behavior to get through a small portion of the task. For most people these suites of intent and movement are processed through the machinery of habit. For me they require intention, attention, strength, and help to work at all.

Getting pants on in the morning is not the

simple matter of putting them on one leg at a time. For starters, I can't do it standing like most people. I have to ask my wife for help while I push myself up using the arms of the wheelchair. Or, I could get them on one leg at a time while lying down, a method that might or might not require as much from assistance from Sheila or an aide.

And, of course, what kind of pants? I need a pair with a long enough rise so when I draw close to the toilet in the wheelchair there won't be too much of a struggle. And what kind of closing? Button-fly is out, zipper is good, but I have to close the top button. Luckily, for this and other tasks we have the devices occupational therapists provide: the button puller, extended shoehorns, sock pullers, grippers. In any case, what takes the typical person five minutes, takes me three or four times as long if all goes smoothly.

But some days, of course, I do not pay attention. Perhaps I am distracted, daydreaming, a little more tired at the end of the day or I have the slightest fever, weakening me just enough. When it comes time to transfer from my chair, I do it "in my sleep." I end up on the floor.

WILL AND WISH

ONE WEEKEND PAST, our Tibetan Terrier was an

especially good reminder that sometimes the willing spirit can overcome the weak flesh. Bodhi had a neurological condition causing vertigo, difficulty with proprioception (knowing where his limbs were—a symptom I share), and ataxic (off-kilter) gait; he also had a hard time with visual focus and depth perception. As a result, he had numerous falls—fortunately, there wasn't much distance between his head and the ground. And he'd get up and go on.

To give him a better grip on the hardwood floor, we got him some rubber dog booties. They were helpful, but couldn't be left on too long. One paw was infected; he wore a sock on that paw and took antibiotics for the infection (something else in common with me). When we took the bootie off his good front paw (where he had more sensitivity, strength, and control), he started licking it more than was good for him. As a distraction and as his due for good cheer, we got a bone out of the freezer. It did the trick.

After gnawing for a bit, he did what all dogs must: Get to the dirt, dig a hole, and bury the bone. So there was Bodhi, big bone clenched firmly in his jaw, a little disoriented with the ups and downs of ramps and a handyman in the backyard, circling around until he found the rich loam in Sheila's garden, falling over, getting up, digging, covering, and eventually coming back in. The day passed and an exhausted Bodhi made his way to his bed. And what did we find there? And how did he get it there? His soil-seasoned victory trophy, his bone.

A sometimes overwhelming sense of fatigue is one of the most familiar symptoms of many chronic illnesses. It may be caused by any one or a combination of factors, such as muscle weakness, spasticity, medication, depression, infection, or a rise in body temperature due to weather, exercise, or too-hot bath or pool water (as is the case with MS). We might be too tired to perform the simplest of daily chores. All sorts of vicious cycles can exacerbate tiredness. Spasticity in my legs interrupts and shortens my sleep, leading of course to greater fatigue, and so on. For some of us, this exhaustion might leave quickly. For others, it disappears once its immediate cause is removed, and unfortunately for some, it is ongoing, perhaps waxing or waning in degree.

The "fatigue factor" accounts for a great deal of the frustration that comes with chronic illness because others assume that if we look well or move without a cane or other aid we *are* well. Even loved ones, not to mention physicians or employers, have difficulty understanding the ways in which fatigue can dim the light of attention. If there is no outward sign of illness, people might tell us, "You look so well," and unkindly perceive us as lazy, neglectful, or unsociable.

I remember when I first used a cane. I had enough strength to walk from a handicap space into a store without much apparent effort, but by the time I came out of the store my difficulty was evident. I recall exaggerating when I first left the car so people wouldn't think I was misusing my placard.

In the early years of my illness, fatigue was listed as a sometimes symptom of MS. Now it is recognized as its chief feature. I wake up in the morning filled with enthusiasm to do something later. But as the day wears on, my excitement turns to a need to summon up reserves or change plans. Fortunately for me, both family and friends understand that our plans are conditional, subject to change or cancellation. But, of course, I want to be active. I want to socialize. I don't want to disappoint my wife or my friends. I want to be alert and present for clients. I want to be and do. What can be done?

First, and perhaps obviously, I have people in my life I wish to be with, a few good friends and family. Secondly, I actively find things I want to and can do. When I could no longer walk or ride a bike, I found a wheelchair bike. Bodhi obligated me to navigate our neighborhood. I started to paint. When I no longer had a studio, I wrote poetry. To warm up to write a third book, I began a mini memoir. To get over dry spells in the book writing, I sketch out blog pieces.

Most importantly, I amend Newton's First Law of Motion that states (more or less): A body at rest will remain at rest unless an outside force acts on it, and a body in straight motion will remain so unless acted upon by an outside force from another direction. *I replace outside force with inside force and that is my will.*

Example: My mind seems wrapped in cotton and my body hung with weights. But as is true of so many aspects of our personality, I have masks to wear on different occasions. On the outside, I appear to be brimming with energy. Often, reality comes to imitate the performance.

Example: I will use language consistent with my wish. I am not *tired*. I wish I had more energy. The genie in my subconscious says, "yes."

Example: I am using a cane. We are attending a play, but parking is far away. I can barely support myself. I imagine a winch with a cord attached at one end to the theatre and at the other to me. I keep the picture in my mind as the winch pulls me through the streets to our seats. I make it.

And so on. I harness my wish to my goal through my will. And I choose to use my will.

CREATIVITY AND ILLNESS

MS IS MY MUSE

"WOUNDED HEALER" IS a phrase that has been used to characterize the shaman of traditional cultures who undergoes a time and trial of suffering as an initiation into his calling as a healer.

> The archetypal wounded healer of classical culture is wise Chiron the Centaur. He was the teacher of Aesculapius, among others, to whom he imparted knowledge of both music and medicine.
>
> Accidentally wounded by Hercules, Chiron could not heal himself. The immortal Chiron would have suffered unendingly had he not offered to die for Prometheus, himself condemned by the gods for his theft of fire. In honor of Chiron's nobility, Zeus granted the centaur the release of death. The mythic resonance between Chiron, Aesculapius, music, medicine, empathy, suffering, and the creative heat of Prometheus suggests that the suffering body and mind are also sources of their own transformations. Imagination and suffering alloy to make something other.

Authors, poets, and playwrights—from Homer, Sophocles, whoever recorded the great

Hindu epics, to any modern artist, whether it be George Eliot, John Keats, Emily Dickinson, Eugene O'Neill, or nearly any composer or painter such as Goya or Picasso—have they not looked clear-eyed at grief, aging, illness, and loss? Great modern myth makers, such as Friedrich Nietzsche, Sigmund Freud, Carl Jung, and Albert Camus tell of the human spirit facing itself naked, alone in a world without the consolations of religion.

The muses (Ancient Greek, perhaps from the Proto-Indo-European root *men-"think") in Greek mythology are the goddesses inspiring literature, science, and the arts. It was said that the winged horse Pegasus touched his hooves to the ground on Helicon, causing four sacred springs to burst forth, from which the muses were born.

Multiple sclerosis is my muse, a visitation from the gods to be shaped and reformed by my own wish and will. In this excerpt from my poem "Transubstantiation," I honor my muse.

As time wastes me and disease sapped powers slip away,
I fear the falcon's swift stoop.
With wary eye and crystal tears, I wheel up the snow packed ramp
to my eyrie and make spells
to keep hooded sadness and savage symptoms at bay
from thirty years of weakness, aches, fevers, fatigue, pain,
missed connections between muscle and nerve.

I craft this poem as antidote to the hard nouns of science
and count on one thousand and one tales of transformation

to shield and sustain me
as myelin shreds and black holes tatter my brain.
I use myth and metaphor for medicine,
swallow fact and fiction, placebos and pills.

I am Hephaestus, twist footed gimp god,
as infant hurled into the sea by mother,
shame ravaged Hera. On bone thin legs
I limp from fire to forge to link fine nets of shimmering gold.
With smithy brawn I hammer swift Achilles' bronze shield
exquisitely thin layered to snap heroes' spears.
I emboss great cups for Zeus' own lips
to touch and drink and shape jeweled cane
to strut my crooked self. In gleaming metal mirrors
my hobbled beauty glows.

My psyche is fed with images that are mine! I imagine myself being kneaded in a slab of dough. The fingers of the baker touch me, inflicting a wound on my legs. My soul is being readied for the baking. Who is the baker? What is the bread? Or I picture my struggle with disease as if I were a farmer, constantly in close touch with local conditions, the terrain my body on this particular day. The farmer cannot be sure when a hailstorm will pour down upon his crops or a drought might blessedly end. He knows that an infestation can plunder his fields and leave him with the even greater labor of gathering up what he can save.

Likewise, I do not know when an exacerbation, temporary or more lasting, could force me to change plans, abandon goals, or even let go of my dreams. The farmer, like the handicapped, works at a different pace from other men. He moves more slowly and with greater vigilance. He notices a little more. Perhaps he is simply grateful for small successes or minor defeats that "could have been worse." I imagine myself that man.

Or imagine that illness is loaded with information. We construe symptoms as the unwanted noise that impedes our aims, viewing the marks and signs of illness as a sort of static that interferes with the organism's intentions and acts. To perceive symptoms as signals and illness as information gives people a chance to break out of the narrow dichotomy of health and disease.

Complex systems are composed of unpredictable and chaotic processes that hide deeper structures of order. What appears to be either predictable or random has been shown to be neither. Instead, there is an order to disorder. Form and structure appear, only to disappear until reorganized into novel patterns once again. Psychologists recognize this process as one of insight that triggers change.

We Do Not Live by Bread Alone

An Asian tale tells us of the master potter whose renown for perfectly formed works spread throughout the land. The emperor, a connoisseur of skilled crafts-manship, demanded to see a display of his wares. The potter demurred, his attention focused more on his craft than on his fame. But the emperor insisted and the master reluctantly agreed. The day came for the showing and his apprentice frantically gathered the pieces for display. The emperor and his entourage entered the potter's shed and were properly astounded by the beauty before them. But one piece, completed just in time for the royal visit, was missing; the potter ordered his student to bring it forth to show.

"But it is cracked and chipped from when I knocked it sweeping the floor this morning," the young man said nervously.

"Yes, my son," the potter reassured him, "but it was perfectly worthy of the emperor when I drew it from the kiln."

"I CREATE," WROTE the artist Paul Klee, ill with scleroderma at age forty, "not to cry." As with water, creativity and imagination will find a way through us to be expressed whether we are disabled or ill. All spiritual, artistic, and philosophical traditions agree that human life is filled with suffering. Some are oriented toward its detached acceptance as an unavoidable fundament of existence. Others suggest that living as rich and good a life as possible despite the inevitability of loss and pain is a more worthwhile path. The traditions also differ on the degree to which whatever God or gods exist care for or intervene in our lives and whether any divine reward awaits the good.

But central to most teachings is the idea that we do not live by "bread alone." It is, of course, important to eat as well as we can. When we think of healthful nutrition, or medication for that matter, we usually mean that which is made from plants, animals, or minerals. The cleanliness of our water and air and certainly how we breathe is also important. Yet "man does not live by bread alone." There are other substances that we take in, metabolize, and express that contribute to transforming us for better or worse depending on their nature and quality. These are the impressions that enter our senses, initiating an amazingly complex firing of chains, nets, and webs of neurons throughout our organism, influenced by the way we consume them, and in so doing alter our minds and souls.

Eye, ear, nose, mouth, skin—each is a portal to our souls. What we see, hear, smell, taste, touch, and believe is as much food as the burgers and kale and grain we eat. How else to explain how certain songs or stories can move us, or a particular conversation or the absence of a touch can leave us curious, enchanted, or bereft? We know, as well, that people can die from a sorcerer's curse and be raised up from despair or depression by a pastor's blessing, therapist's counsel, or friend's comfort as effectively, if not more, than by any pill.

Our senses are hungry for experience as well. Our skin craves or delights in touch. Our mouths and ears wish to speak and listen simply for the pleasure of being what they are. We sniff the air, cock our ears, tap our feet, lick our lips, rub our hands together, keep an eye out. It may seem odd to describe sense organs as active creatures, conscious beings, but who would argue that, at times, this or that body part has a life of its own and on other occasions they work together to compensate for injury to a limb?

When you speak to me, waves of air inhaled by you in the room where we both sit emerge from your lungs and throat in variable pressure waves influenced by the affect and meaning you intend to convey, and reach my ears, stimulating nerve cells processed by my embodied mind, itself a mist of mood and anticipation. In turn, I respond, the waves of meaning made of air expelled from me, swirling about as do the sonic clashes of rock guitars or tuneful harmony of a classical suite. Depending on what and how and where we speak, sing, chant, or pray, we may eat well or poorly. Perhaps the symposium of Socrates, the last supper of Jesus, and the Passover Seder had symbolic and liturgical roots in this felt socio-neuro-biological fact?

There is a karmic destiny to the art we make and respond to, the words we speak and hear, the textures we touch, scents we inhale, and what we bring to our lips. What is called sacred architecture, mandalas, robes and chants, ceremonies and psalms are composed with that knowledge and intent. In Jewish tradition, children began their Torah study by writing and tasting Hebrew letters of honey. This is truly the erotic, pervasive, passionate connection between bodies and souls that hopefully gives birth to something new, an intellectual conception rather than simply a biological one.

We effect and are affected by conversations and creations that took place millennia ago and will take place in years to come. They can wound and heal, make us worse or better, drag us to hell or raise us up, answer some questions or cause us to question our answers. All these images are molecules spinning through us from generation to generation. Our personal memories generally span only three generations. We experience something of the emotional reality and personality of our grandparents; to learn about their parents we rely on their memories or stories. The stories we in turn make up and pass on to our families create a karmic web that transcends time or, perhaps, defines it. Culture is no less material than our genes. Both art and medicine change us. One leaves something finer behind.

Art, of course, cannot offer either the creator or the viewer a guarantee of escape from suffering. At times, sorrow can only be endured. Much art, ordinary as well as great, exists as a memorial to those whose voices were strangled or stilled. Nevertheless, art can bring the possibility of healing to those living with illness. It gives form to that which is unspeakable, renders coherent the shattered and broken. Just as illness can be a vitiation of experience, art can give it both spirit and flesh. Art is a medicine for the suffering we call illness, as it may function similarly for those afflictions known as meaninglessness, despair, poverty, abuse, exile, and war.

There are goods that illness delivers to us as well as the more obvious harms. Making contact with the capacity of imagination to generate new ways and possibilities of being is an event of significant healing importance. Is it possible that as we draw symptoms and meanings into a new relationship our illness itself can become a source of our own healing? Prickly sensations and peculiar signs that once brought fear are now also objects of curiosity and potentially "food" for thought.

I hope we can begin to see how our creative imagination is a potential bridge between the world of too much suffering and one of denial and no suffering at all. It serves as a middle ground, an empty space, a *terra incognita* that is filled with undiscovered continents and terrain. From this place that is not a place, we can draw images, metaphors, and sensations that give meaning, manageability, and shape to our voices and worlds within.

ART AS HEALER

A PROFESSOR OF mine, Abraham Maslow, describes a psychology of value that is what philosophers, poets, and artists have long known. To flourish as an individual, it is necessary to have certain goods in our lives. Just as we need vitamins to be physically healthy, there are values we must have to live well. Experiences of truth, beauty, justice, order, richness, playfulness, and meaningfulness are all food for the soul. Without them, we are vulnerable to the sicknesses of cynicism, bleakness, mistrust, depression, grimness, and despair.

Suffering increases when people living with chronic illness are deprived of important nonmaterial values. Lives are more constricted and sickness worsens when there are fewer opportunities to participate in and enjoy the making of beauty or the study of truth. Music, gardening, reading, and viewing nature are all therapeutic. No one lives by bread, work, or medication alone. When we are sick, the body pushes its way into the mind, insisting on its own agenda. Doing art, the mind enters into the body, searching for the elusive sensation that will yield the next word, stroke, or note. Creative activity provides the opportunity and means to remake the fruitful interaction of body and mind once again.

The idea that art itself can be a healing experience is something the ancients knew, but until recently, modern healers often treated occupational, art, or musical therapy as busy work for patients that permitted them to express their pathology in a socially acceptable way. It is only now being acknowledged that art can directly affect disease. Art enables individuals to knit together new kinetic melodies and meaning in the face of the unraveling of movement and order that chronic conditions incur.

We sing with our whole body. We use posture, breathing, the diaphragm, the sonic structure of the "mask" that gives our tones resonance, the feelings and thoughts we express to make our song. The self-as-voice reveals itself through sound. The same is true of painting. It is the hand that grips the brush, but the artist who places pigment on canvas. The firmness of the stroke, the response to light and color, the leaning toward and back from the work, the turning of the head to catch an angle, these are acts of the whole person, not of the hand alone.

Writing is also an organic process. The writer searches for a word "on the tip of his tongue," tenses a fist, or wiggles a hip to capture just the right phrase, and he tunes into his gut to judge how well he has conveyed his meaning. The singer, painter, or sculptor no less than the author senses in his or her body for the proper note, tint, or plane. Throat, eye, and hand are not passive tools of the mind to be used for a purpose that is not their own. They are mind itself.

Plato was wary of the effects of literacy upon memory. Monastics worried that the mechanical reproduction of the Gutenberg press of holy texts would deprive scribes of the benefit to their souls from the binding of hand and eye by prayerful attention in the copying of sacred works. The very word *religious* comes from the Latin *religare*, to bind, a reference to the disciplined commitment required for such work. Traditional movements ranging from the iconographic gestures of Hindu and Buddhist mudras, as well as the practices of the Sufi Mevlevi order known as "whirling dervishes," are other examples of the unity of spirit, body, and mind.

Imagine that illness is a legitimate way of being, a local world like deafness or blindness. Think of the stiff gait of a person with Parkinson's, the labored breathing of one with emphysema, the explosive bursts of speech and twitches from those with Tourette's, as dance, song, poetry. Illness moves to a different tempo than we hear in the world of health. Imagination is a middle way between realities too harsh or wearing to bear, yet too insistent to be shut out.

The image offers a place at the table to the chronic illness, an uninvited but nonetheless unavoidable guest. We search for symbols evocative enough to permit us to conceive of new possibilities, just as a rock cleared from a cave mouth allows a thirst-quenching stream to flow. What if we approach the illness experience as a work of art, a dramatic epic, for example, with moments of farce, terror, catharsis, and pity?

THE ESTUARY

I WRITE POETRY, and as a swimming fish in a local small pond, I've done quite well with prizes and recognition. I am sometimes asked where the idea for a poem comes from. I answer, "a seed image," a sight, a word, a feeling that ripples, flows, and grows until something is left that may be quite different from what was present at the source. An "estuary" is the seed image for what follows.

An estuary is the changing border where salt and freshwater mix. It's a place of variety, perhaps where amphibious creatures first moved from sea to land. Like the hypnagogic line between wakefulness and sleep, it can be a source of creativity and inspiration. Chronic illness often brings with it an estuarial consciousness that moves from body focus to outside environment to internal state. We can learn to use this liquid state, one that others see as pathology, as a gift to help free us from fixed ways of belief and open us to richer ways of being.

The imagination is rooted in the body, and each possibility has its own feeling. In the creative process, for example, one continually dips into the personal reservoirs of images and associations embedded in deeds, words, and memories. Different metaphors evoke distinct complexes of thought, emotion, and attitude. Poets especially are conscious of the physicality of language, including the literal force of punctuation. Poems spoken aloud, to oneself or another, are not the same works when scanned quietly. Reading is also an activity of what John Dewey called the "live creature." The eye lingers over the shapes of letters and words; the body senses the effects of dialogue, plot, and style. Art is alchemy. Through art the distress of illness can be changed into something more valuable.

An almost involuntary mindfulness mixing with free floating sensory vigilance, estuarial consciousness differs a great deal from the ways our attention was placed or attracted in our pre-diagnosis everyday lives. Over time and with practice, we may learn to navigate the currents and tides of our personal odyssey without quite knowing what adventure or challenge next awaits us. Postures, gestures, and movements are not simply aids to prayer or meditation in consciousness traditions—they are the practice itself. Both thinking and speaking are embodied. They do not occur in something called the head/brain distinct from the body. Mind and thought are expressions of the whole being.

The surge of the body into consciousness and the strong emotions evoked by loss, uncertainty, and change awaken associations and fantasies linked to primal fears and yearnings for security and coherence. In self-defense, symbolic and meaning-making capacities are animated. The organism attempts to reorganize and find new pathways for identity and expression. When enlivening metaphors or opportunities for creative action are not available, however, the energy of adaptation and change is dampened. Loss without mourning cuts short our human potential for healing and transformation.

THE PORTUGUESE MAN OF WAR

The Portuguese man of war is not a single multicellular organism but a colonial organism made up of specialized minute individual organisms called zooids. These zooids are attached to one another and physiologically integrated to the extent that they cannot survive independently and function as if they were an individual organism. [Wikipedia]

AND SO ARE we. We are flowing rivers, rippling

streams, transforming with each breath. We are legion. Our being, or *beings* as we shall see, is different as are the beings of all and everything in relation to us. And illness conjures up different beings and different worlds.

For example, the being of stairs and our being with stairs have particular qualities and meanings, most of them unconscious, when we are young and learning to navigate them safely. Stairs are physical challenges to be conquered, literally one step at a time. They are also places of risk and possible fall or injury that might bring on parental scolding or comfort or both. Stairs may lead to the hospital.

They are sources of pride. They are places to sit and hide, perhaps to overhear adult conversation or spy on grown ups' behavior, parties, misdeeds. The tops and bottoms of stairs have different feelings and even moods. For a child, a stairway is a path to mystery, through which sounds descend from the top or rise from the bottom, or it is a journey to the warm and welcoming smell of a kitchen below or a grandparent's apartment above. Stairs are, as it were, vertical doorways, liminal spaces between states of being.

When I was about eight, our stairway was a place of ambush where I could wait silently until my brother passed by and then leap upon him. Outside or in, others used stairs as shelves for mail, flowerpots, sneakers, and boots. Banisters are slides in some homes, stairs an indoor playground. This is just a fraction of what a staircase is for a child; its being has deep physical and intellectual roots spread widely in memory, sense, and feeling.

As adults, our stairways are generally not particularly special. If I live in a home without one, however, a part of me may miss it, may hunger for it, without any conscious nostalgia on my part. Its absence may drive me to look for a house with two floors. I might feel irritation or get into irrational fights with my partner independent of home design, but evoked by something that awakes "stairway being," with as much reality as any other "I" perceived to be myself. I do not mean this metaphorically. The stairway being will look like me, except for highly differentiated, distinct yet meshed networks of reaction. He will be one of a number of beings, all with different memories, needs, and desires.

"Food beings" are another powerful example for many of us. "I" love ice cream. I often describe it as a food of the gods. It can be eaten by all people—young or old, with or without teeth—and invariability people are happier for it. It contains many of the basic pleasure food groups—sugar, fat, chocolate, and caffeine. It supplies quick energy.

I have many positive childhood memories of

ice cream in all kinds of situations and even now I top off most evenings with a Klondike bar. I would have a very difficult time if I were on an eating regimen that did not include ice cream. Certain beings might indeed be screaming for ice cream. They might dream of ice cream, think of cheating, start rationalizing why a change of eating habits would be a good idea. I would be jonesing.

Now, back to stairs. As I glided up and down stairs through my younger years, they were largely emotionally invisible to me. When I became ill and increasingly disabled, I began to notice them with a wider range of feeling. They became obstacles rather than ways of passage. Instead of simply moving up and down them, I now had to plan how to negotiate them. At different times I had to use this or that device to help me climb or descend them. Where I went, and whether in fact I *could* go, depended to a great degree on whether or not there were stairs. I saw stairs everywhere, where before they were used and fell out of mind. It was as if they had barely existed, like the flashlight in the drawer doesn't exist until its absence or the failure of its batteries impresses its presence upon us.

These days we live on one floor and I use an incline plane—a ramp or covered stairs—to exit and enter. Stairs are different beings for me now, and I am inhabited by different beings as well.

Before there were frequent falls and calls to EMTs to restore me to my chair. Since we have moved to one floor, however, and more recently installed an overhead lift, I have not had a fall.

So, as a child I saw stairways brightly, and then dimly if at all, but now stairs and so many other things are lit. Different worlds embodied by a constantly changing gathering of meanings, beings, and Is, some lost, now found. Amazing grace!

DEATH

DROP THE CURSED PETTINESS

TO BE MINDFUL of death is a common precept in all religious and consciousness traditions from East to West and through the centuries. In various Buddhist teachings, monks gaze upon a dead body or skeleton and reflect, "My body is no different than the one I behold." It is even said that some teachers told students that if they meditated without awareness of their own mortality the effort would bear little fruit.

Imagining the future is central to human existence. The angels in Wim Wender's extraordinary films *Wings of Desire* (1987) and *Far Away, So Close* (1993) reside in eternity. Their one wish is to know what it is to be human. The wish cannot be granted unless they fall into time and subject themselves to the possibility of unfulfilled desire or the yearning passion for *again* or *more*. Unlike angels, we are faced with the impossibility of a limitless horizon and so must choose.

Central to critic Harold Bloom's argument for the importance of a literary canon is the fact of our passing from this world in three score and ten years. Had we double that time to read, he suggests, there would be less of an imperative to mark out those masterpieces that one *must* read.

The ability to defer present and immediate gratification for future satisfactions is typically considered a significant measure of maturity. When we make a prudent decision on behalf of our children or grandchildren we may rarely or never see, we feel proud and grateful for the opportunity to do so. One of the pleasures we enjoy as parents is daydreaming with children, partners, or friends about what lies ahead. We fantasize about how we will be as parents, what our children will look like, the kinds of lives they will lead. Indeed, we conceive our offspring imaginatively before we conceive them in flesh.

The approach to the future of our living with illness is a makeshift process that reflects the uncertainty and changes in conditions, diagnoses, resources, and support that cannot be avoided. Most of us make ongoing adjustments during our lives and attempt to plan for that which might or might not come to pass. We hold on as long as possible to the fundamental assumptions that support our confidence or fears about what is to come.

Socrates's manner of meeting his own death as recounted by Plato ought to be the ideal toward which a philosopher aspires. Indeed, Socrates and later the Stoics considered the dispassionate contemplation of one's own death to be a means of achieving greater self-control and freedom from fear. Remember, these were people for whom death from battle, pestilence, or accident was much more likely than in our own time and place.

Early Christians used the phrase *memento mori*, or "remember you must die," as a means to help both pious and more ordinary folk turn their attention away from the vanities of this world toward the greater and eternal rewards or punishments of the next. With the arrival of the plague, the imminence and pervasiveness of death could not be ignored. Still life paintings included a newly shot hare or pheasant among living fruit or plants—a reminder of the brevity of life.

In Islam, the "remembrance of death" is an important signpost to be heeded among the many tempting pleasures of life. The Mexican Day of the Dead is a compound of Catholic and indigenous ritual and imagery. Recall Don Juan's teaching to Carlos Castaneda that "Death is our eternal companion" and his injunction to "drop the cursed pettiness that belongs to men who live their lives as if death will never tap them."

In our time and place most of us are not well situated to view skeletons, skulls, and the dead. But we with chronic illness are "better off" than most to contemplate our falling apart. Illness, rather than Death, is our most visible companion, but unless we live in a state of denial of "mortality salience" (a fancy term for the recognition of our inevitable death), it's hard for us to ignore it. I'm unlikely to die sooner from multiple sclerosis than a "healthy" person in my age group. But I am at greater risk for a UTI, and, if resistant to antibiotics, that could kill me. I don't need ashes on my forehead as a dust to dust reminder. A wheelchair and the everyday reminders of what I must do to stay clean and healthy are enough.

IMPERMANENCE, COMPASSION, AND MR. HOLMES

SHEILA AND I saw a wonderful movie, *Mr. Holmes*, with Ian McKellen and Laura Linney. The setting is rural England shortly after World War II. The elderly Holmes has retired from detective work and the burden of celebrity he left behind more than forty years earlier.

He lives with a housekeeper and her twelve-year-old son, a boy on the verge of adolescent arrogance. As his memory fails, exacerbated by a series of small strokes, Mr. Holmes makes an effort to correctly recall his last case and why it led to withdrawal from his work, as well as a total estrangement from Watson.

Throughout the film in a variety of situations, Holmes continues to insist, as he did in his career, on the importance of facts and dismisses the relevance of emotion. He has sought a number of cures for his senility—ranging from taking cocaine, to keeping bees for royal jelly, to visiting Hiroshima's devastated ground zero to find a particular medicinal plant. Paradoxically, through his growing attachment to the boy with whom he reluctantly begins to share his apiary knowledge, Holmes gradually remembers his last case. He contributed to the avoidable death of a young woman by failing to provide her with comforting lies; instead he laid out her case in full, harsh clarity. Previously so dismissive of Watson's fictions, Holmes begins to see the pleasure and comfort they gave so many in a terrifying and irrational world.

As Holmes physically and mentally weakens, aided by the dissolving comfort of the sea, shame and guilt press upon him. Through his increasing affection for the boy, he realizes the knowledge and reality of impermanence must be supported by the grace of compassion. Holmes acknowledges the lack of warmth and relationship in his life. Fortunately, his opening to feeling does not come too late. It is a profound, shall I say Buddhist, or simply human film.

THERE IS NO MAP FOR GRIEF

THERE IS NO map for grief, there is only memoir and it is tattooed onto the body. Mourning is a profoundly upsetting physical experience as well as a felt emotion. Our hearts are broken; the loss is tearing us apart; it is gut wrenching; I'm all choked up.

We know that the smallest loss can unleash a tidal wave of sorrow and tears; one is rarely prepared for the reality of experience. I was not ready for the possible impact of our beloved dog Bodhi's passing on my already compromised body.

For example, during the two weeks preceding his death, I went through two rounds of antibiotics for a serious urinary tract infection. My nurse visited three days after to take a sample to check if the infection was gone. She asked where Bodhi was, and when I told her we tearfully shared the grief as she had lost her own dog the year before. She took my blood pressure and it was the highest I've ever had measured. She took it again before she left and it had dropped nearly thirty points, but it was still unusually high for me.

The days following the painful decision were filled with the tears that accompanied it, as well as writing, reading, and responding to the many, many expressions of sympathy along with accompanying sorrow, nods, and smiles. Unfortunately, episodes of gastrointestinal distress accompanied the UTI.

Were these the result of continuing infection, the antibiotics, the festive meals we had with (coincidentally) visiting family, simple symptoms of multiple sclerosis, the bodily expression of grief, a combination of all these, or some other factor? Clearly, the experience and expression of sorrow is a tangled knot.

It's the nature of a force more powerful than God: Lord Time. In some Hindu traditions, Kāli is the greatest of all the gods and Brahma, Vishnu, and Shiva all arise from her like the constant waves in the seas and ceaseless time, inexorable in its passage and unstoppable flow.

Human memory is its greatest enemy by building monuments and memoirs from its detritus and deposits. Memory gives us feelings and recollections to hold onto, to know I was there, or I lived and loved. Yet, it also leaves us vulnerable to the pain of recalling what we have lost and will lose as time pulls us, willingly or not, onward into its devouring maw. As we age, we often think how recent the long-ago past seems to be. And clearly, this present moment will similarly pass and the future, no matter how far in the distance it appears, will soon arrive.

On the one hand, *carpe diem*, seize the day. On the other, *tempus fugit*, time flies. All things must pass, and, writes Leo Tolstoy in *War and Peace*, "There will be today, there will be tomorrow, there will be always, and there was yesterday, and there was the day before".

I began this ramble of thoughts on memory

and loss soon after our beloved Bodhi died. I was limited in my ability to be distracted from my grief. I couldn't take a walk or exercise; no movies at the mall because I was sick. Worse, there was no Bodhi to care for or play with. I was reminded of the research reporting that many people experience illnesses within a year of the death of a dearly loved family member or friend. It is as if a hole has been torn in our souls. And I surely know that many, many people are in worse situations. At least I was cared for and cared about. The measure of love is perhaps, at times, reflected in the depth of our grief.

It is important, as well, to remember that mindfulness or the realization of impermanence is not intended to suppress feeling, but to open us to our shared humanness and, therefore, to compassion. We can say that tears, blood, and milk are symbolic representations in art, as well as our bodies, of the liquidity, the movement of life.

SO GLAD TO CRY

FORTY YEARS AGO, I was one of the first clinicians at the newly established mental health unit at the local children's hospital. Most of the kids I saw were from economically disadvantaged families in great distress. What could I offer these children in one hour a week? I was happy to see them. I enjoyed talking with them about what they liked about their lives and listening to the troubles they were willing to share. Apparently they looked forward to seeing me as well.

Gradually I realized that the little I gave was something that meant a great deal to them: genuine attention. My interest in them was real. There were no therapeutic techniques or strategies that actually could affect their difficult lives. But I believe that these kids—with very difficult lives at home, school, and in the streets—and I felt pleasure simply being present with each other. Eventually, however, under the accumulation of hearing so many tales of too-hard young lives, I moved on. But I was glad I cared for them enough to cry.

"MS sucks!" Laughter and nodding heads greet my opening statement. It is twenty years ago and I am facilitating a workshop for individuals and families living with multiple sclerosis. Participants are pleased that a professional who shares their diagnosis has a similar perspective on their situations. Group discussion is lively, but then a fellow about forty years old says something that gives me pause.

"Not that I'm glad that I have it [MS]," he remarks, "but I've become a better person since I was diagnosed ten years ago." His comment sounds familiar: I realize that several other participants have pronounced much the same thing. Each has described a personality change since the onset of illness that would be considered a worthwhile outcome of any psychotherapy process. One woman says she has become stronger, more self-reliant. Another claims she is less negative than before her diagnosis. A man states that he is more intimate and emotionally expressive in his personal encounters. Others in the group nod their heads in agreement.

Irvin Yalom reports similar findings in his work with terminally ill cancer patients. Many people, he writes, describe "startling shifts" that "can be characterized in no other way than 'personal growth'." Among the changes people identify are "a rearrangement of life's priorities," "vivid appreciation of the elemental facts of life," "fewer interpersonal fears," and "enhanced sense of living in the immediate present."

Yet, despite these warrants of significant and positive change, every single person in my workshop makes sure to add, "Not that I'm glad that I have it." Why are people so reluctant to say they are glad to have experienced something from which good has been made? Of course, for some with illness, the losses are too recent or too great. They may fear worse days to come or feel unable to wrench any meaning from their fate. Yet it is possible for people to find or even imagine value where there appears to be none.

And so it is, as the recent loss of our dog Bodhi sadly reminds me. There is no love without suffering. And I am glad I suffered and cried, for it means I loved.

ALI, "A TRULY FREE MAN OF FAITH"

"Life is the clause within eternity, between the two commas that are birth and death."

—*Bobby Shuman, 7th grade, 1960*

"The pattern isn't visible until the carpet's fully woven."

—*Robert Shuman, 1996*

I WRITE THIS piece with the awareness of the two poles of our humanity recently displayed. The first aspect of our nature was horribly displayed by the evil massacre of more than fifty people in Florida. Of that, I have no more to say then may blessings of peace in good time rain upon them, the wounded, and all of their families and friends.

The second side of our nature, and of particular relevance to us who live with chronic illness or disability, is highlighted by the death of Muhammad Ali, and more importantly, the manner of his being during his extraordinary life. Born with magnificent physical talents, he carried what were and in many ways still are burdens of race, color, and class. He transcended these limits. Ali was an exemplar and embodiment of the better possibilities of being human, developed in body, mind, and heart. He was, in my opinion, with all his faults and flaws, a saint.

As is the case for traditional virtues, many of the conditions for self-actualization are consistent with a recognition of limits, imperfection, and humility; they have little to do with progress, individuality, or health. What makes Ali so extraordinary is that he met the criteria for self-actualization at a relatively young age, when name change, due to his religious conversion, was met with nationwide anger. It was especially marked by the principled stand he took against the Vietnam War despite the many injuries he suffered as a result. Yet he remained committed to his path of resistance. And despite his youth, scorned and attacked by powerful government and business interests, he expressed his ideals with passion, intelligence, calm, and escalating amounts of goodwill.

"I think he decided," said Bill Clinton in his simple yet deeply perceptive eulogy, "before he could possibly have worked it all out, and before fate and time could work their will on him, he decided he would not ever be disempowered. He decided that not his race nor his place, the expectations of others, positive, negative, or otherwise would strip from him the power to write his own story."

And then Clinton flipped our usual way of thinking of a life's course and certainly of an athlete's. "I will always think of Muhammad as a truly free man of faith. And, being a man of faith, he realized he would never be in full control of his life. Something like Parkinson's could come along. But being free, he realized that life still was open to choices . . .

"The first part of his life was dominated by the triumph of his truly unique gifts . . . we should all be thrilled, it was a thing of beauty. But the second part of his life was more important. Because he refused to be imprisoned by a disease . . . he perfected gifts that we all have, every single solitary one of us have gifts of mind and heart. It's just that he found a way to release them in ways large and small.

"So I ask you to remember that," President Clinton went on, "we all have an Ali story. It's the gift we all have that should be most honored today, because he released them to the world, never wasting a day that the rest of us could see anyway, feeling sorry for himself because he had Parkinson's...but, with a free spirit, it made his life bigger not smaller...a free man of faith sharing the gifts we all have. We should honor him by letting our gifts go among the world as he did."

Old and New

A NEW GOD has come into our lives and home. Kai, a Tibetan Terrier like Bodhi of blessed memory, from a most kindly breeder. And just in time for the days when grandson Caito is not there for palling around.

The last two months have been a great time to be reminded unwillingly of the phrase associated with chronic illness, "sick and tired of being sick and tired." Two months of one long UTI (or of recurring ones) equals eight weeks of antibiotics and probiotics. And just when I thought I'd killed it, it began again. My doctor agreed at my request to try out a prophylactic antibiotic that, of course, has its own serious possible downside, making the bacteria for which the medication has been effective more resistant! This was similar to when I had my lovely monthly dosing of steroids to tamp down inflammation and minimize immune responses (the foundation of MS, an autoimmune disease), but which had the unfortunate accompanying effect of lowering the immune system and then making me more vulnerable to infections, which of course initiated a heightened immune system response. But I did love that weekend of steroids, going without sleep, bursting with clarity and creative production. Of course on Mondays I crashed, but it was worth it.

In any case, there we were on Father's Day in

the emergency room at 2:00 to get a CAT scan, rather than attending a wedding on the Cape. I gave them a urine sample when we got there. At 6:00, two great pieces of information. The first, to a dehydrated me, "Oops, we spilled your sample!" and the second, from the ER doctor, "If you were sent here to get a CAT scan, you go straight to radiology. If you're here, we decide what you need."

Things moved along from there as quickly as possible and we emerged from the hospital to a beautiful summer night of the solstice, full moon shining. And once again, lessons in patience, living with uncertainty, and many others—all of which Sheila carried off better than I did.

As for Kai's first day, he was mellow and playful with ball, duck, and stick. At night, he lay in his crate crying until we covered three sides with towels, put on light classical music, and slept until all of us were awakened by birds. The next day, rest with an around the block walk that he did magnificently, followed by sleep. A wonderful pup!

ALL ILLNESS IS FAMILY BUSINESS

THE YOKE OF RELATIONSHIP

One day, according to the Sigalovada Sutta, the Buddha saw Sigala immediately after his morning bath bowing to the east, the south, the west, the north, above, and below. Following tradition, Sigala had practiced this ritual daily since hearing of his father's death. When the villagers observed this ritual, they honored the gods who lived in the six directions. As a result, good luck, happiness, and prosperity were bestowed upon on the people.

The Buddha revealed to Sigala what the six directions represented. The east stands for the parent; the south, the school teacher; the west, one's spouse; the north, one's friends; above, the spiritual mentor; and below, one's employer or employee. Each direction represented a fundamental human relationship. To honor the six directions was to recognize the mutual responsibilities in each of these roles and to vow to fulfill them as we move through life.

ONE CHARACTERISTIC OF a religious attitude is the recognition of an inseparable relation between the very small—ourselves, our egos—and the immeasurably large—a god, nature, the universe. Just as the ocean cannot exist without its drops or the desert without grains of sand, so there can be no greater without the lesser, no death without life, or mind without a body. The Sanskrit term *yoga* has its root in *to join*, associated with the imagery of the yoke connecting a team of oxen. So we humans are joined to something greater, perhaps the vast field that our master the farmer plows, as well as to each other.

As previously mentioned, the word *religion* has a similar meaning at its Latin source: *binding*. Long ago, monks, or the religious, were bound by monastic rules. Our illness, binding or limiting us in so many ways, provides constraints upon our self-will. Perhaps we wish for the same focus to bear the years of illness with dignity and grace.

If we think of ourselves as religious, spiritual, or travelers upon a path, we are bound to not only an abstract greater, but to values expressed in relation to ourselves, others, and a larger whole. Perhaps the most common factor in all religions or traditions, even those for whom there is no divinity outside of man or woman, is a version of the Golden Rule. It is said that the Dalai Lama, when pressed to describe the god of Buddhism, replied, "My religion is very simple. My religion is kindness."

Both Rabbi Hillel and Jesus said the essence of their teachings was in the relations between people, the Golden Rule. Clearly, to treat with respect or kindness those whom we might feel deserve our wrath or disgust is not a simple or easy thing. It may at times call for a reach beyond the limits of our ordinary being. In some cases, we may think that only some sort of saintly or angelic being could do it. Illness and disability alter our lives, by choice and by fate, inside and out. Fortunately, they can serve as a medium through which we work to connect with ways of being that are ultimately good for ourselves, others, and the world. The wound heals.

All illness is family illness. We are deluded to think otherwise. If I suffer, my family suffers. If anyone in my family suffers, I do as well, in ways that may not be apparent but are nevertheless so. The same is true, of course, in my relationship to the larger world and its connection to me. The evidence for the interdependence of all is clear in the environmental crisis and its consequences of war, poverty, and disease. Truly no person is an island. Unfortunately, but understandably, that you or I might change the larger world in a visible way seems so far beyond our resources that it is difficult to even imagine what we might do if we had the opportunity.

At the same time, we acknowledge that in our absence, the greater world would be different, perhaps even diminished. In some traditions, our role as humans is to transform lesser energy into higher states for the sake of the greater whole of which we are a part. Our task is to take what is given, whether it appears to be for better or for worse, and change our fate into something finer. It is that vow which makes any committed or enduring state—marriage or illness, for example—a sacrament, a voluntary acknowledgement of limits to ensure the time necessary for the distillation of suffering matter into soul and spirit.

BURDENS OF CARE

FOR THE LAST few days I've had an infection that has required a great deal of physical care and attention from Sheila. It is easy to forget how much of the burden of care falls upon a spouse. In fact, Sheila's graduate dissertation addressed the emotional and physical consequences that injured the so-called "well spouse."

I am fortunate that I have a team of competent and lovely regular care providers who come to my house. As soon as my physical therapist picked up my increased spasticity and I emailed information on my symptoms to her and my physician, they instituted a care plan that included five providers coming to the house today to initiate care and ease some of Sheila's load.

What is particularly noteworthy about my situation is just that—easing Sheila's load. Much is made of the technological revolution in medicine and the impersonal nature of most hospital-based medical treatment. The fact is, however, that our society is undergoing an enormous shift in the way technology is used to care for those with chronic illness. Homes and families are expected to function like medical settings at the same time that hospitals are attempting to bring the family into hospital care.

The romantic notion of the orientation toward care of most traditional cultures takes place under the nurturing eye of Hestia, goddess of the hearth and domesticity. Traditional home care reflects the unity of family, neighborhood, parish, and other voluntary associations ensuring some degree of mutual support in times of need. It has long been assumed that mothers or daughters would bear the burden of giving care. The assumption that hands-on care is within a woman's sphere is accompanied by the expectation, often unmet, that husbands and sons bear the financial obligation to keep the household functioning and to maintain insurance or reserves to meet medical costs.

When the goal of home care was primarily palliative, aimed at reducing the immediate suffering of someone who was ill, the treatment was usually an extension of what was already done within the home—cooking, laundering, companionship, helping with small chores, and occasional trips out to the doctor, the hairdresser, or visits with family and friends.

Even when done with the best of intentions

and love, people are often unprepared for some of the physical, emotional, and financial conse-quences of providing extensive, as well as intensive, care at home for those with chronic illness. The movement of health care for the chronically, seriously, or terminally ill person into the home can be a form of exploitation and unexpected hardship, playing upon the desire of a family or individual to give comfort to the ill loved one within the intimacy and security of the home for as long as possible.

At the same time that they must continue to cope with the ordinary and often stressful tasks of everyday life, family members have to perform complex, frightening, intrusive, and painful procedures on their child, spouse, partner, or parent. Formerly, such medical interventions were either not available or carried out in medical settings only. It is one thing to change soiled bed sheets or assist someone in the bathroom. It is another to replace a tracheotomy tube in the throat of a child who is dependent on a ventilator for life support or to supervise the use of an infusion pump for a parent's cancer.

What is the carrying capacity of the home environment? How much of a load can primary caregivers and individual family members bear? Time, a limited resource, is especially inelastic to those who must carry out all the tasks of caregiv-ing as well as other daily roles. Taking care of individuals with illness at home has never been easy, but it is made even more difficult when expectations change about who will provide treatment and how.

FAMILY ETHICS

IN THE 1990s, I was a student at Harvard Divinity School. My interest was moral philosophy, sparked by the kinds of situations I encountered in my therapy practice. There were occasions, custody issues for example, in which I was asked for opinions or recommendations. Rarely were cases clear-cut. Children and their parents experienced painful gains or losses no matter what I proposed. I thought it impossible to be in my position without acknowledging the "blood on my hands." What I owed was a thoughtful process and an open ear and heart to all parties.

Browsing in the old Harvard Bookstore on in the pre-Amazon days, I discovered Martha Nussbaum's brilliant and profound *The Fragility of Goodness: Luck and Ethics in Greek Tragedy and Philosophy.* She explored the suffering often associated with being forced to choose between two goods or identify the "lesser of two evils" when negative consequences will befall the unchosen—think *Sophie's Choice* or Patrick's dilemma regarding custody of Amanda at the end of the 2008 film *Gone, Baby, Gone* for contemporary illustrations. These are situations where the costs of either choice, regardless of the benefits, are terrible. Yet a choice is forced because failing to choose is itself a decisive act. Nussbaum discusses the questions of whether one can be called a good person if harm is the unavoidable outcome of well-intentioned and essentially necessary acts.

Often we and our families find ourselves in situations that call for us to exercise what I call moral intelligence, among them the increasingly complex judgments we need to make, where the outcomes are inevitably mixed and which we approach with marked ambivalence. This often arises when we decide on the distribution of resources and caregiving.

To what extent can family members be asked to sacrifice their interests for our sake? What if our families do not share our values? To what degree do the claims of the obviously suffering person deserve more consideration than the claims of others? How often do the lengthy and intrusive assessment and search for the best and most rational solution create more unnecessary pain?

In the past, for example, custody decisions were made in the best interest of the child. After many years, people realized the time, money, and effort involved in deciding what was "best" inflicted unnecessary pain on child and family. The standard now is less "best" and more "reasonably good."

How often do we admit that there is no perfectly good, wise, or just solution to many medical quandaries? Is it any wonder that the deep feelings that surround our own experiences get stirred up and hurled into these whirlpools of emotion? In circumstances where we must decide between incommensurable goods, things that cannot truly be compared, where we face adversity and the hard judgments that may be required by ill fortune, maybe the best we can do is know who to turn to so we can examine the perplexing questions.

Families have always engaged in moral discourse when confronted by the challenges of chronic illness. They cannot avoid addressing the ethical and moral judgments and dilemmas that are such an important dimension of the illness experience. Individual and family questions about who is responsible for whom, for example, are at the heart of defining a family's ethos. Its everyday moral vocabulary includes should and ought, commitment and responsibility, owing, shame, tragedy, and pity.

Families not only join together in moral conversations, with all the passion and pain that serious situations evoke, they also demonstrate in a mostly unheralded way the four classical virtues of courage, *phronesis* (practical wisdom), temperance, and justice. We show courage as we accept and withstand the losses and suffering that are common companions to illness. We exhibit a sense of justice when we make the inevitable choices about the allocation of resources, whether of time, money, or attention.

People struck by misfortune are commonly forced to select among incommensurable goods as they attempt to salvage something from their previous lives. How can one quantify who is more deserving of this or that support, aid, or companionship? Family members demonstrate phronesis when they decide whom to include in their conversations about proper care and how to develop and follow through on a sound course of action. Temperance is the virtue on display when individuals and families attempt to balance all these concerns and share the weight of their burdens. The language of virtues is a lovely one with which to reflect upon and discuss how people attempt to solve the difficult problems in their lives.

In Erik Erikson's psychosocial view of personal development through the life cycle, for example, the first step in building character is identity formation. The ability of our family and community to help us through our developmental crises lays the foundation as we age for the emergence of hope, will, purpose, competence, fidelity, love, care, and wisdom. Our family, then, is a moral and ethical milieu in which we learn from each other a sense of fairness, reciprocity, generosity, and commitment.

We find ourselves in families, whether one or many, bound by ties of kinship, marriage, intimacy, and responsibility. Receiving life, care, and opportunity from our parents, participating in the give and take of family life, expressing vows of marriage and fidelity, bringing children into the world, initiating and sustaining friend-ships, and drawing new people into the web of family relations—these are among the many events that confer ethical obligations upon ourselves and others.

WE ARE NOT RATIONAL ACTORS

WHO IS FAMILY? When I ask people whom they consider to be family, the common response is, "It depends." In a conversation with Sheila, I gave a quick definition of family as "people whom I particularly care about and toward whom I feel greater obligation than others." I added that I am more intimate with many friends than I am with some family members, but that I am likely to assume greater responsibility for the latter in times of crisis or need. Sheila, on the other hand, stressed the qualities of interdependence and intimacy in characterizing family. She was put off by my term "obligation" because it implies acting from a sense of duty rather than out of what she called a "wish."

To the Romans of classical times, *familia* referred to the "house and all belonging to it." Just as many families do today, Roman families considered domesticated animals to be part of the family. Relationships between children and their dogs, cats, or horses, and memories of those ties, can easily generate more emotion and meaning than the connections between siblings.

Many burdens befall our families as we live with chronic illness, aside from the obvious ones of increased demands on resources of money, time, and physical energy. An unexpected stress is the way chronic illness raises the issues of family membership and participation. Questions of who is in or out are more important than they seem at first glance. Discussions about who is a member of the family are not of minor importance: they can influence in crucial ways both the nature of the illness experience of the person diagnosed and the possibility of illness among others as well.

Some of us consider certain people who are related by neither blood nor marriage to be family and expect reciprocity of feelings and responsibilities from them. Godparents and unofficial uncles and aunts often have this status. Thinking of a family as a fixed entity hides its diversity and flexibility and the ways in which family members function within and between networks. It plays down individual differences within a family—as well as the rich connections that many people have with a number of different families—and imposes on it concepts that often do not resonate with the ways its members make sense of how they live.

I find the concrete images and metaphors of braids, ladders, tapestries, and gardens helpful in working with individuals, couples, and families. Questions about current and older friendships and acquaintances are often as helpful as ones about family of origin, particularly when families must identify potential sources of short- and long-term support. Relatives frequently give enormous help in times of acute crisis, but their visits may be intermittent if they live far away. Families may want and need to use friends who are closer by.

"What is the right thing to do?" and, "What kind of person (father, mother, son, daughter) do I wish to be?" are moral questions. In the course of everyday life, our behavior implicitly poses such questions, with little reflection on our part. It is through the answers we receive, from others as well as ourselves, that our character, self, and family are formed.

Our families are the places where we first learn and express our character. My family is a social space where we learn and practice ways of caring, make sense of what is worthy of honor, and confront shame. In our families we learn—or not—from each other a sense of fairness, reciprocity, generosity, and commitment.

In most people's encounters with chronic illness, making moral judgments is not an abstract process. The arguments that break out between family members, between friends, and even within ourselves, are usually ambiguous and more crucial to living through the illness experience than the thinner cases discussed in medical and ethical journals. In our families, decisions are made and actions taken that may not be in the best economic interests of either individual family members or the family as a whole. Parents willingly make monetary sacrifices for the sake of their children. Many of us and our family members give up our own needs for individual achievement or remain in difficult relationships for the sake of more vulnerable others. We are not, from the point of view of economic theory, "rational actors."

THE SO-CALLED "WELL SPOUSE"

A very difficult few months of caring for Bodhi and me (with several infections) as well as maintaining her practice, our household, and her roles as Nana, *wife, and friend, remind me that Sheila's own voice from her 1998 Pacifica Graduate Institute thesis should be heard once again. **Also, let it be noted we are in our fiftieth year of being together—and nearly the fortieth year of her sharing my illness.***

A BIOMEDICAL MODEL that often fails to discriminate between disease and illness tends to ignore the psychosocial and spiritual dimensions of illness. The spouse's role is reduced to an instrumental one for the purposes of caretaking, treatment compliance, and, increasingly, providing medical services in the home. Regardless of her own needs, the spouse's willingness and availability is taken for granted as an economical alternative to private nursing care.

Naming one partner in a marriage as "sick" or "disabled" and the other as the "well" spouse serves neither. First, it creates a false dichotomy of two people living in two different realms, but forced to coexist. This accentuates the differences between them, rather than focusing on shared suffering and mutual need. Second, it reinforces the role of the diagnosed partner as the passive and dependent member in the relationship with a lesser ability to control or influence his or her life.

Third, it promotes unrealistic expectations of the so-called well spouse, to be the stronger, more active party in the partnership, the intermediary and voice in the outer world, responsible for the "weaker" partner's physical and mental wellbeing, and obligated to maintain the family and household's functioning. Fourth, as a carrier of the family's overall load, the well spouse is the one who worries that he or she isn't doing enough, caring enough, or providing the right kind of help, and frequently feels guilty when the ill partner does not recover.

The felt suffering of the non-diagnosed spouse, unrecognized and often dismissed, is usually pushed underground. To complain would be to lift the veil, revealing a harsh reality behind the guise of smiling sacrifice and right-eousness. People often say to those enduring the often private, less visible effects of chronic illness, "But you look so well, how could you be ill?" The question and answers may easily be the same if directed to well spouses.

To honor and acknowledge the reality of the lives and losses of millions of so-called well spouses the world over, we think it better replace the earlier term with the phrase "non-diagnosed" partner or spouse. Any view of illness as trans-formative must be grounded in the dirt of actual lives and experience.

The combination of unpredictability, progres-sive loss over a lifetime, and no hope of cure make chronic illness devastating for even the most well-adjusted couples. In that sense, the diagnosed person has the disease, but both people in the relationship share the illness. In fact, the illness may be worse in some ways for the caregiving spouse than it is for the so-called sick partner.

Society provides a partner with a disease with a sick role, which does have some benefits. He or she is expected to rest, stay home from work, reduce the level of activity, be waited on by others who attend to his comfort and care. The non-diagnosed spouse has no complementary role which is clearly sanctioned or feasible. She must simultaneously be a wife, nurse, mother, spokesperson, head of household, career woman, financial manager, nutritionist, maid, physical therapist, social director, and cheerleader.

While attention, treatment, sympathy, and support are focused on ill partners, their non-diseased spouses are expected to muster the strength and carry on with few complaints and little support or acknowledgement. The super-woman myth has nothing on that of the caregiving spouse.

The multiple losses, changes in daily living, new roles, and multiplying demands take a toll on even the most saintly of so-called well spouses. Many report severe anxiety and bouts of clinical depression as a result of living with the constant uncertainty, dashed hopes, and enormous weight of being the primary witness and caregiver to their partner while juggling career and family responsibilities. The cost in lost productivity and opportunity, as well as the sheer emotional, physical, and financial drain equals, if not surpasses, that of any chronic physical illness.

Almost 20 years ago, a plea was made for the recognition and classification of "caregiver disorder" as a treatable psychiatric syndrome deserving of medical and psychological attention. Modern society needs to broaden its vision to perceive illness in a more contextual framework as was pointed out more than half a century ago, "The family is the unit of illness because it is the unit of living." In some ways the experience of living with chronic illness can be compared to abduction into the underworld as in the story of Persephone. The youthful maiden is out in the field picking flowers when the ground suddenly opens up and Hades, her abductor, the terrifying God of the Underworld, takes her below.

As the earth swallows her, Persephone wonders what is to be her fate in this world where skeletons and rotting corpses surround her in the darkness. Before this encounter with Hades, Persephone was innocent and protected. From this point on, she bears the knowledge of the good and evil of existence, and realizes her emotional and physical vulnerability to what lurks beneath the apparent security of everyday life. Persephone is now "twice-born."

As I continued to sift through the stories of spouses living with the partner's chronic illness for my thesis, I went into a period of anxiety and depression that threatened to paralyze me. I tried to move forward with the work, but couldn't. The suffering was calling me down into it.

For a few weeks I gave into my own sadness, anger, and despair, unable to see my own resources or potential positive outcome. I threw myself into my counseling work, spending hour after hour listening to my clients' stories of trauma, abuse, and neglect. I found something healing in sitting with them and being fully present for their suffering. It brought me back to my own experience of severe clinical depression six years earlier.

I had been working long hours as a corporate consultant to extremely difficult and powerful clients who were resistant to change. I felt and fought each day as an uphill battle in which I had to constantly prove myself. Eventually, I became ill and had to have my thyroid gland removed. The wound became infected and did not heal properly. My doctor did not monitor my hormone levels to adjust to the physical changes. As a result, I fell into a deep depression that came on like a freight train going 100 miles per hour. I was unable to work, drive, cook, read, talk on the phone, or make the smallest decision. The only thing I could do was be with myself.

I began therapy and dealt with my feelings about my husband's illness after ten years of hating it and trying to go on in spite of it. It took an incapacitating illness of my own to shock me into stopping my ceaseless rat-on-a-wheel efforts. I learned about limitation and woundedness, what I can control and what I can't. I began to discover a new freedom to drop the things I didn't care about and focus my limited energies on what was most meaningful and nourishing to my soul. I learned a tremendous amount during the nine months it took me to heal and can look back now on that frightening time as a gift to myself.

I experienced directly the healing power of quiet, stillness, and being alone with myself. I found myself drawn to nature in a very powerful way. I created a wonderful woodland meditation garden for my husband and an ever-changing perennial garden for me. Working in my garden, I felt my heart open and a sense of wonder and mystery stirring my soul. I became more sensitive to birds and butterflies, creatures of the air, planting things in the ground to attract them. I felt connected to the elements of sun and sky, earth and rain. Each plant or bulb became one of my offspring and I cultivated and nurtured them with great care and attention. I watched some plants die and others come to life. I saw the cycle of creation and transformation in the soil before me.

As I first was pulled directly into my suffering

and then drawn out from it to connect with the larger world, my depression lifted and my perceptions changed. To do this, I had to let go of the useless suffering surrounding my pain, accept the reality of what was happening to me, and stop wishing I was living under different circumstances. From that position one can say, "Okay, here I am. Now what? What can I make of this?"

IS LOVE JUST A FOUR-LETTER WORD?

TO GRASP HOW our individual selves and families respond to loss is crucial to maintaining a more conscious engagement with our experiences of illness. Shortly after I posted an excerpt from Sheila's dissertation on the "well spouse" on my blog, a reader asked whatever happened to the suggestion that caregiver syndrome be classified as a psychiatric diagnosis. In fact, there is a code: F43.0 acute stress reaction, or R45.7 state of emotional shock and stress, unspecified, which is the code also used for battle exhaustion and other extremely stressful situations.

In one sense, it is an honorable recognition of the daily struggles of caretakers for us, the ill or disabled. On the other hand, it is an example of not fully appreciating what people like Sheila must bear for years, even decades. Researching combat fatigue, I discovered that the US Army determined about 180 days of battle to be the limit of most soldiers' endurance before they were significantly at risk of acute stress reaction. Imagine how many days or even decades of "battle" Sheila is exposed to and wishes to survive, in all respects, intact.

Take the days before and after Bodhi's death during our holiday "vacation." Out-of-town family members we love were staying with us and Sheila was preparing breakfast, lunch, and wonderful dinners. I had my ongoing infection, which required additional daily help from her to manage. She cleaned up Bodhi's accidents and changed the absorbent pads he used in his last week. On Monday we called Roto Rooter to take care of a clog we thought was caused by the usual suspects—roots, from the two giant Norwegian maples out front. That seemed to work.

But Tuesday, as people took showers, Sheila did an unpleasant load of laundry, and I could only sit beside Bodhi, water started seeping up from the shower drain, across the bathroom, and into the bedroom. Every beach towel was laid on the floor. And then the washing machine stopped working.

Eventually another sewer service did the job right; the appliance guy figured out the washer; Sheila amazingly cleaned the floors and gathered up all the wet towels into huge plastic bags. At the same time, she was, of course, grieving in anticipation of the vet's last visit. And my infection was not knocked out (it ended up requiring an intravenous antibiotic emergency room visit four days later). Imagine her concern.

Of course, some people are in much tougher situations. But the emotional and physiological consequences of such stressors over the long term can be quite similar. The body eventually becomes exhausted in its attempts to maintain balance under threat, and health problems and—perhaps worse—depression and anxiety can set in.

So Sheila does her best to maintain a positive attitude, calm, and patience while keeping a beautiful home, working as a therapist, being a loving and generous friend, Nana, mom, and wife. There is so much to say about other consequences of illness upon the well spouse and the importance of acknowledging their needs as well as those of their ill partners. At this moment I can only echo Lou Gehrig's words upon his retirement from baseball due to ALS, "Today I consider myself the luckiest man on the face of the earth," that she is my wife and so gracefully carries her sorrow and compassion for the unavoidable weight of my illness.

Within any home, social space, or office, certain voices are less likely to be raised or heard than others, especially during the often hurried encounters of the medical setting. We can make the effort to listen to others' distress, as well as to what remains unmentionable or is only suggested. Changes that may be medically or therapeutically necessary for me may increase the burden on an uncomplaining Sheila.

Many caregivers who feel ashamed to grieve for the loss of a pleasure, or guilty about how minor that loss seems compared to the disability of the patient, may never speak of it. Family members may naturally not tell of the losses they incur. They may feel obliged to surrender their claims on pain or even their own need to fulfill other family responsibilities.

When illness arrives on the scene, the possibility of psychological cacophony is quite high as inner and outer voices struggle to be heard and others search for silence and hiding. We who are ill—as well as the "well"—need to really listen.

Justified or not, what often frustrates me is when people tell Sheila, "You need to take care of yourself," whatever that means. First, it's an empty remark unless they offer concrete ways or help to do that. It's as if people think love or caring is simply a feeling. Love and care are just four-letter words unless I see the acts that the emotions are intended to motivate. Second, it demonstrates a lack of knowledge or sensitivity to the systemic reality that individuals don't have illness, families do, and every action has rippling consequences.

When we lose touch with the distinct suffering of the souls of individuals and families, we run the risk of being swallowed by the values and ideology of the collective. On the other hand, the good that may come from some calamities, including the opportunity to be generous or helpful, is often what is most difficult to perceive.

72143116R00110

Made in the USA
Columbia, SC
13 June 2017